ENGLISH FOR BUSINESS SUCCESS

BUSINESS ACROSS CULTURES

Effective Communication Strategies

Laura M. English • Sarah Lynn

Longman

Business Across Cultures:

Effective Communication Strategies

Longman, 10 Bank Street, White Plains, NY 10606

Photo credits: page 112, © 1992 McDonald's Corp.;
page 115, courtesy of Blue Diamond Growers

A publication of World Language Division
Editorial director: Joanne Dresner
Acquisitions editor: Allen Ascher
Development editor: Françoise Leffler
Production editor: Nik Winter
Text design: A Good Thing
Cover design: Curt Belshe
Cover illustrations: Sarah Sloane
Text art: Sarah Sloane

Library of Congress Cataloging-in-Publication Data
English, Laura Monahon.
    Business across cultures / Laura Monahon English, Sarah Lynn.
        p.   cm.
    ISBN 0-201-82532-5 (pbk.)
        1. Industrial management—Cross-cultural studies. 2. Corporate
culture—Cross-cultural studies.   3. Communication in management—
Cross-cultural studies.   4. Negotiation in business—Cross-cultural
studies   5. Intercultural communication.   I. Lynn, Sarah.
    II. Title.
    HD38.E473 1995   94-35166
    658—dc20   CIP

    4 5 6 7 8 9 10-CRS-98

To Andy and Sam for their eternal patience, love,
and ability to always make me laugh when I need it most.
L.M.E.

To Celoni, whose love and support have accompanied every step.
S.L.

CONTENTS

NOTES TO THE TEACHER

Overview

Using the case study approach, this book explores issues in cross-cultural communication in the business context. It is designed for intermediate-level ESL (English as a second language) students who are in the business field or are studying business, or who are simply interested in cross-cultural conflict and resolution. The text employs a great range of communicative activities, including the case study approach, information gaps, interviews and role-plays to encourage students to think critically, solve problems, and develop their oral communication skills. The activities are supplied with cultural information from many countries so that students can compare their own ideas and traditions to those of people from other cultures. This makes the text interesting and fit for use in both the multicultural and monocultural classrooms.

Because of the nature of the content and the student-centered style of the activities, the book can be used from a lower-intermediate through advanced level. No previous knowledge of business is required.

Warm-up

A cartoon introduces each unit. The questions that follow prompt students to share their knowledge or experiences related to the topic.

Case Study

The cases are either authentic or based on extensive cultural research. They provide students with realistic contexts in which cross-cultural misunderstandings occur while also presenting useful business concepts. The case study approach invites students to think about cross-cultural conflicts in a specific way and grounds the student discussions to realistic solutions.

Students may read the cases and complete the comprehension questions and vocabulary work in class or at home. It is important, however, that students talk about the case together and complete the making inferences section together before they embark on the problem-solving section. Working together allows students to identify the problems and see the many possible perspectives to what could seem a straightforward case.

Problem Solving

Students read different pieces of cultural information that help them better understand one point of view on the conflict presented in the case. These readings are scattered throughout the appendix to ensure that students read only their own assigned material. Students then pair up with someone who has read other information. Together they try to construct a whole view of the misunderstanding in the case.

Using the newly acquired cultural information, students are then asked to develop concrete plans to help solve the conflict in the case, and ideally will reach a synergistic solution. These plans can be presented in class or be left as written presentations.

Around the World   This section has a twofold goal: to broaden students' basic business knowledge and to draw on the students' own experiences and cultural perspectives. It expands on the business and cultural topics first touched on in the case study, providing cultural information about many countries through minicases, graphs, tables, and short readings. Students compare their own experiences and traditions in interviews, discussions, group projects, or class experiments.

Language Expansion   This part of each unit gives the students the opportunity to practice the vocabulary in the topic area of the unit. The first section presents a set of idioms or expressions related to the unit topic. They are presented in connection to a theme or metaphor (*time is money*, or *negotiations are a sport*). This approach helps students see how cultural attitudes are reflected in language usage.

The Word Forms section provides the students with further practice of the vocabulary introduced throughout the unit. The word forms presented were chosen because of their consistency in meaning. They are not the only possible derivations. The class may want to go beyond the book's treatment of word forms to explore the many varieties of meanings that spring from one word.

STEREOTYPES ACROSS CULTURES

Unit

1

1. What stereotypes do these people have about each other?
2. What stereotypes are there of people from your country?
3. How do we get stereotypes? Where do they come from?

DO WE UNDERSTAND EACH OTHER?

The following are two letters, both written by employees of a British-based international public relations firm. The two employees work together as editors.

To the Editor-in-Chief:

I am writing you to tell you of some problems I have been having with the other editor in the office, Sakiko Fujita. We don't work well together. She seems to depend on me for most all the ideas and decisions. I seem to carry the responsibility all the time.

To give you an example of our **tensions**, I will describe what happened between us today. This morning we were working on an article. I found that I was doing all the work. She didn't contribute to the discussion. When I finally asked her what she thought of my decisions, she **hesitated**. Then she only said that she thought my work was interesting and she would think about it more. I am very **frustrated**. She doesn't give me her opinion or ideas. How can I work with someone who doesn't communicate or give **feedback**? I want to move forward with our work but I can't with her. How can I get her to take on more responsibility?

I know that part of the problem is communication. She doesn't seem to listen to what I am saying. She rarely looks at me when we speak. And she sits so far away. She is a very reserved person. I **can't figure out** what is going on in her head.

I hope that you can talk to her and get her to be more involved in our work. As things are now, our **collaboration** is not at all productive.

Sincerely,
Edmundo Montaya Reyes

My Dear Friend Noriko,

Hello. How are you? I hope everything is going well. I am not doing so well. Life at GTP International has been difficult lately. One of my **colleagues** is very difficult to work with. He seems only to **consider** himself. He doesn't know how to share work space or work responsibilities.

Part of the problem is that he has difficulty listening carefully to people. When we work together, he rarely asks me for my opinion. He just talks all the time! When I try to offer my opinion, he interrupts me. For example, today we had to make some important changes in an article. He told me what he wanted, and when I tried to say it wasn't the best idea, he just didn't want to listen to me.

I feel a bit uncomfortable with him. He sits very close and looks at me all the time. I try to get some distance between us but he just pushes closer. He doesn't give me room to talk or think. I think his **behavior** is a little aggressive.

I don't know what to do. Maybe I should ask for a transfer to a different office. It is too hard for us to work together. I don't think we can **resolve** our differences. Tomorrow I will mention my problem to the editor in chief. I think she will understand.

Thanks for listening to me and my troubles.

With love,

Sakiko

Vocabulary

Match the following words (taken from the two letters) to their definitions.

_____ 1. tensions

_____ 2. hesitate

_____ 3. frustrated

_____ 4. feedback

_____ 5. figure someone out

_____ 6. collaboration

a. think about

b. a person you work with

c. working together

d. way of acting

e. opinion in response to someone or something

f. understand someone

_____ 7. colleague

_____ 8. to consider

_____ 9. behavior

_____ 10. to resolve

g. to clear up a problem

h. feelings of worry, pressure, or anger

i. to pause

j. annoyed and disappointed

Reviewing the Case

Underline all the complaints Sakiko had about Edmundo in her letter and all the complaints Edmundo had about Sakiko in his letter. Put the complaints in the correct categories in the chart.

	Sakiko Says	**Edmundo Says**
Eye contact	_He looks at me all the time._	_She doesn't look at me when we speak._
Physical distance		
Cooperation		
Giving opinions		
Listening		

Making Inferences

In the situation described above, there are two people from different countries working together. They each have their individual style, personality, and experiences, but they also have *cultural expectations*. They expect other people to behave according to their own cultural ways. For example, Edmundo expects Sakiko to look at him while they speak to each other. In his culture eye contact is an important part of communication. When she doesn't frequently look him in the eye, he thinks that she isn't listening to him. He understands her behavior according to his culture's rules. But Sakiko is acting in accordance with her own cultural rules. In her culture it is common to look away frequently while speaking and listening. She expects him to also look away from time to time. When he doesn't, she feels uncomfortable with him.

Read the following list of expectations. Decide which are Edmundo's (*E*) and which are Sakiko's (*S*). Share your answers in groups. The first one is done for you.

<u> *E* </u>   1. When people are working together they usually sit close to each other. Closeness indicates interest and cooperation.

_____ 2. A man should give a woman some physical distance. Physical distance shows respect for a person's space

_____ 3. People should invite each other to say something in conversation. One should ask questions or remain silent so that the other person has a chance to say something.

_____ 4. One should begin speaking even if the other person is speaking. If one doesn't interrupt, one will never speak.

_____ 5. Silence expresses disinterest or boredom.

_____ 6. People often disagree with each other. It is normal to have different opinions.

_____ 7. People should give their opinions and not wait to be asked. It is the individual's responsibility to say what he or she feels.

_____ 8. One should express disagreement carefully. An open disagreement could offend or embarrass someone.

_____ 9. It is not polite to speak while someone else is speaking.

_____ 10. People may be silent for a few seconds if they are thinking about something. One should respect the silence and not interrupt it.

_____ 11. If there is a conflict, one should try to resolve it indirectly so that no one is embarrassed.

_____ 12. It is impossible to resolve a conflict without facing it directly.

Problem Solving: Simulation

You are the editor-in-chief. You want to keep both Sakiko and Edmundo because they are both excellent editors. How can you help them resolve their conflict? With a partner, talk about a possible solution. Write out a plan of action that will help the two employees resolve their differences. Think about the following questions:

1. Why are Sakiko and Edmundo having problems with each other? What specific behaviors are causing the misunderstandings?
2. What small things can they do to work together better on a daily basis?
3. What is the best way for you, the editor-in-chief, to communicate with them? Should you write them each a letter? Or should you call a meeting with both of them?
4. How much should you, the editor-in-chief, be involved in their cultural misunderstandings?

Discussion

Read your action plan to the class. As a class, discuss the advantages and disadvantages of each solution. Consider the following questions:

1. Does the solution consider each employee's cultural style?
2. Is the solution feasible for the two employees?
3. How will the solution affect their future relationship?
4. How will the solution affect the work environment and other employees?

AROUND THE WORLD

Values A value is the belief that a certain part of life is especially important. Every culture places different emphasis on family, work, religion, and love. Some cultures value family loyalty and romantic love. Other cultures emphasize independence from family and hard work. Still others emphasize religion and honor in the community.

Your Point of View

Individually, think of four values that are important in your culture and four values you think are important in the United States.

My List	
My Culture	**American Culture**
_____	_____
_____	_____
_____	_____
_____	_____

Form small groups of students from your country. Share your lists and decide which four values are most important in your culture and in American culture.

Group List	
Our Culture	**American Culture**
_____	_____
_____	_____
_____	_____
_____	_____

Discussion

Share your group's list with the class and compare it to the lists made by students from different countries in Appendix Activity 2. Answer the following questions as a class.

1. Do groups from different cultures choose different values to describe American culture? What are the differences?
2. What do their descriptions of American culture tell you about their own culture?
3. What influence does your own culture have on the way you see people from other cultures?
4. How can you see people from other cultures without a bias from your own culture?

Stereotypes vs. Cultural Generalizations

A stereotype is a belief that all people from a culture behave a certain way. It is an opinion based on one's own cultural values and prejudices and on little information about the other culture. For example, a woman from a culture that values hard work looks at a people from a fictional land called Zibi. In Zibi, people work at their jobs about five hours a day. So, the woman says, "People from Zibi are lazy." This is a stereotype because she states that every person from Zibi is the same and it is an opinion based more on the woman's own values than on any thoughtful observation of Zibian values or lifestyle.

In this book, we talk about different ways of doing business. We make cultural generalizations about different styles of business. This does not mean that every person who lives in a particular culture will do business in a way that fits the generalization. Within each culture there are many choices. There is, however, in every culture a standard way of doing things. The cultural generalizations describe those standards and the values that guide those standards. For example, one could make a generalization about Zibians and say, "People in Zibi usually work about five hours a day. They spend the rest of the day taking care of family and farming. Family life is highly valued." A generalization is based on observation, not prejudice. It explains the standard practices of a culture but does not determine how every person in that culture behaves.

Applying Your Knowledge

With a partner, discuss the difference between a stereotype and a cultural generalization. Then read the following statements about the fictional country called Zibi. Decide which are stereotypes (*S*) and which are cultural generalizations (*G*). Circle the language that makes some of the statements stereotypes.

_____ 1. Zibians are selfish.

_____ 2. In Zibi gifts are often presented at the end of a negotiation.

_____ 3. It may take two or three days to get an appointment with a Zibian.

_____ 4. Zibians never let you know what they are thinking about. They always try to confuse you.

_____ 5. In Zibi, many businesspeople invite their colleagues to their homes for dinner to talk about work.

_____ 6. Arriving on time in Zibi usually means arriving ten minutes after the agreed time.

_____ 7. In Zibi nothing runs on time.

_____ 8. It is common in Zibi to discuss every detail of an agreement before signing a contract.

_____ 9. In Zibi, all the power in a corporation stays at the top. You can never get a middle manager to make an independent decision.

_____ 10. Zibians spend too much time eating.

Responding to Stereotypes

There are many ways of responding to stereotypes. The following Asian-American encounter illustrates that.

AN ASIAN–AMERICAN ENCOUNTER

An American man attending an international relations banquet was sitting across from a man who looked Asian. He wanted to start a conversation so he asked the man loudly and in very simple English, "Like food?" The man politely nodded yes, but said nothing.

During the dinner program, the master of ceremony introduced the Asian-looking man as an award winning professor of economics at an important university. The professor was invited to give a short talk about world trade issues. After a short discussion in perfect English the professor sat down. He then looked across to his neighbor and asked loudly and in very simple English, "Like talk?"

Discussion

Answer the following questions and share your answers in groups.

1. What stereotype did the American have about the Asian-looking man?
2. How did the Asian-looking man respond to the stereotype?
3. Do you like the way he responded to the stereotype? Why or why not?
4. Have you ever been faced with stereotypes? How have you responded?
   a. with anger at the person
   b. with anger at the stereotype
   c. with a joke
   d. with an explanation of why the stereotype is wrong
   e. with silence
   f. _____

LANGUAGE EXPANSION

Expressions and Idioms

When we talk about people from other cultures we often express our understanding or lack of understanding. Here are some of the more common idioms that express understanding or inability to understand. Match the idioms with their definitions.

_____ 1. to catch on

_____ 2. to be beyond someone

_____ 3. to see

_____ 4. to read between the lines

_____ 5. to hear someone out

a. to be too difficult to understand

b. to understand

c. to begin to understand

d. to listen to someone and try to understand despite one's own anger

e. to listen carefully and hear what is said and left unsaid

Complete the following sentences with the correct idioms.

1. Most training programs give the trainees a few months to _____ to how the business works.

2. That new computer program _____ him. He just doesn't understand the most basic applications.

3. It is important to _____ even when you are angry. Many communication problems develop because people just don't try to listen to one another.

4. That is a very well-marketed product. I can _____ why it is so successful.

5. When negotiating with people from other cultures, it is important to consider everything carefully and to _____ . What someone does not say is often as important as what one says.

Word Forms

Often the same word base can be used in verb, noun, and adjective forms. Complete the following chart with the missing forms.

Verb	Noun	Adjective
behave		
	collaboration	collaborative
consider		considered
	frustration	frustrated
generalize		generalized
prejudge		prejudiced
respond		responsive
tense		tense

Complete the following sentences with the correct verb, noun, or adjective form of the words in the chart above. Use one form of each word base, and do not repeat any words.

1. They fired her after she yelled at the client. Her_____ was rude and inappropriate.

2. She stopped smoking last week. It is now impossible to work with her. She is too _____ to do anything.

3. He listened to her ideas and then said he would _____ using some of them.

4. Learning how to speak a new language can _____ even the most patient student!

5. They are quite a team! He has great creativity, she has lots of technical knowledge, and they _____ well together.

6. She was confused by his question, so she didn't _____.

7. Some people see a couple of American movies and then _____ that all Americans are violent.

8. _____ prevents people from seeing one another with open minds.

MAKING INITIAL CONTACTS ACROSS CULTURES

Unit 2

1. Where is this French businessman? Does he look relaxed? What do you think he is feeling?

2. Have you ever arrived in a country without any knowledge of the language or without knowing anyone?

3. If you wanted to do business with a certain company in another country how would you want to be introduced? Look at the list below and decide what is a good idea (G) and what is a bad (B) idea.

_____ Write a letter introducing yourself to an appropriate person in the company.

_____ Call and introduce yourself to an appropriate person in the company.

_____ Make an appointment to introduce yourself to an appropriate person in the company.

_____ Ask an influential person to introduce you to someone in the company.

_____ Contact the chamber of commerce, consulate, or other official agency and ask for an introduction.

CASE STUDY

GETTING CONNECTED IN COLOMBIA

A bank in Bogota, Colombia decided to improve its computer communications system. The top sales manager of a young but successful communications company in the United States wanted to get the Colombian **account**. The sales manager, Peter Knolls, was a young man with an excellent **background** in computers and U.S. sales. He had been one of the original partners in this small communications company.

From his office in Chicago, he started to look for the right person to **contact**. He called several people in the Colombian bank but wasn't able to **get ahold of** the person in charge of the account. He decided to call the Colombian Association of Banks. The association coordinates bank business and encourages foreign investment. It also acts as a **third party** to introduce foreign contacts. An agent of the association named Roberto Coronas as the **key contact** of the Columbian bank for the account. The agent then suggested they all meet together in Colombia. Knolls, wanting to be certain that a trip to Colombia would be worthwhile, asked the agent for Coronas's phone number and called him immediately. He introduced himself to Coronas and began to explain how his company could develop the best computer system for the bank. Coronas suggested they meet each other in person to talk further.

Before leaving for Colombia, Knolls sent a brief letter to Coronas describing his company and its interest in doing business with the bank. He also sent his company's **credentials**. These included a **profile of his company** with all the necessary financial information from the past two years and some **references** from satisfied clients. This information would show what a good **reputation** the business enjoyed in the United States.

Knolls went with the agent to meet Coronas in person. After a brief introduction, Coronas suggested that the two men have dinner together that evening. At the dinner the sales manager was ready to talk about business, but Coronas wanted to talk about general topics, such as business friends and Colombia's literary and cultural history instead. Knolls said his interest was in business, not in the arts. The young man explained how he had independently developed a successful communications business without any special help or **connections**. He did not **make a good impression** on Coronas.

At the end of the evening, Coronas said they should stay in touch, but he never contacted Knolls again.

Vocabulary

Circle the words that are most similar in meaning to the words in italics (taken from the story).

1. A young but successful communications company in the United States wanted to get the *account* to develop a new computer system for the bank.
   - **a.** businessman
   - **b.** money
   - **c.** job

2. He had an excellent *background* in U.S. sales.
   - **a.** experience
   - **b.** time
   - **c.** interest

3. Peter Knolls started to look for the right person to *contact*.
   - **a.** touch
   - **b.** speak to about the business
   - **c.** be friends with

4. He called several people in the Colombian bank but wasn't able to *get a hold of* the person in charge of the account.
   - **a.** understand
   - **b.** hug and kiss
   - **c.** speak to

5. This association acts as a *third party* to introduce business contacts.
   - **a.** independent group
   - **b.** large dinner
   - **c.** businessperson

6. The association identified Roberto Coronas of the Colombian bank as the *key contact* for the account.
   - **a.** person who introduces
   - **b.** person who gives information
   - **c.** most important person

7. He sent the company's *credentials*.
   - **a.** description of qualifications
   - **b.** credit cards
   - **c.** description of beliefs

8. These included a *profile of his company* with all the necessary financial information from the past two years.
    a. picture of the company
    b. description of the company's history and accounts
    c. description of the company's employees

9. He also sent some *references* from satisfied clients.
    a. dictionaries
    b. letters recommending the company
    c. products

10. This information would show what a good *reputation* the business enjoyed in the United States.
    a. standing or position
    b. look
    c. history

11. The young man explained how he had independently developed a major communications business without any special help or *connections*.
    a. family
    b. knowledge
    c. friends with power

12. He did not *make a good impression* on Coronas.
    a. make an imprint
    b. paint a nice picture
    c. have a positive effect

Reviewing the Case

Answer the following questions and share your answers with a partner.

1. What did Peter Knolls, the U.S. sales manager, first do to find out more about the Colombian bank?
2. How did Knolls get introduced to Roberto Coronas, the Colombian banker?
3. What kind of information did Knolls send to the bank before the first meeting?
4. What did Coronas want to talk about over dinner?
5. What did Knolls want to talk about over dinner?

Making Inferences

Answer the following questions and share your answers in groups.

1. Why do you think it was difficult for Knolls to contact the right people over the phone?
2. Why do you think Knolls sent information about his company before the first meeting?
3. Why do you think Coronas invited Knolls to dinner?
4. What was the purpose of the dinner for Knolls?
5. Why didn't Knolls make a good impression on Coronas?

Problem Solving: Information Gap

Peter Knolls is wondering why Roberto Coronas never called back. You are to investigate the different cultural backgrounds of the salesman and the banker. Then develop a plan of action for the two businessmen.

Divide the class into two groups: A and B. Group A reads the Colombian cultural information in Appendix Activity 8. Group B reads the U.S. cultural information in Appendix Activity 5. After reading the information, complete your part of the chart below. Next, find a partner from the other group and ask questions to complete the chart.

	In Colombia	In the United States
1. Is it more common to contact people and get information in person or on the phone?		
2. What are some ways to get introduced to a company? Which way is most common or effective?		
3. In making initial contact, which is more important: the company or the person representing the company? Why?		

	In Colombia	In the United States
4. How important are personal connections? Why?		
5. How much time is spent on getting to know each other? Why?		

Discussion

Go back to your groups, look at the completed chart, and discuss the following.

1. Now that you have more information about both cultures, do you want to change any of your answers in Making Inferences on page 20? Discuss your changes if any.
2. What difference in the two men's business styles had the most impact on their first contact?
3. After that first dinner, what could Knolls do to improve relations with Coronas?

Written Reflection

In this case Knolls was selling his services to Coronas. To what extent do you think he, as the seller, and Coronas, as the buyer, should try to adapt to each other's culture?

Write a plan for Knolls and Coronas so that their first contact is more successful. Your plan should lead up to and include the first meeting. To help you prepare your plan, review the issues in the above chart. When you have finished, share your plan with the class.

AROUND THE WORLD

As is clear from the case study, different business cultures have different ideas about how an initial contact should be made. Different business cultures also use different types of information to determine whether a company is worth working with. Here are two other examples of how to get connected in other business cultures.

Egypt

In Egypt, the government is usually the customer; private businesses usually do not have big international accounts. A good introduction in Egypt requires governmental references. For example, an American businessman in a large company in Arizona, United States, wanted to do business in Egypt. His company had no history of working in the Middle East. He had to get letters of reference and introductions from a U.S. senator and the U.S. government's envoy (government contact) to Egypt before the Egyptians would consider doing business with his company.

The social relationship that develops between the two business parties is also very important. The social relationship is not limited to the one person in charge of the account. During the first meetings, the same respect and social interest should be shown to all persons who are in the key contact's office, even if they are not directly involved in the business deal. These people may influence the key contact's opinion.

South Korea

It is best to make the first contact with a Korean company through a third party. If this method is chosen, it is important to contact a highly respected Korean. South Korea has a clear social structure. People work with people who are in their own social level. In high business circles in South Korea, everybody knows everybody. An introduction through a well-connected individual will open many doors. High-level government officials are the most effective contacts because they can promise some governmental cooperation. The government has a lot of influence on business in South Korea. There are also many trading companies and banks that successfully introduce foreign businesspeople to Korean businesses.

In Korean society, a person's status is defined by education, family, place of birth, current address, friendships, connections, and the size of the company. When businesspeople are introduced in South Korea, it is important that they give personal information about their own connections and education along with the company profile. People sometimes give biographies (a short description of their life) to provide additional personal information. All this information should be given before the first meeting so that the people involved have a chance to learn about each other.

Applying Your Knowledge

Read the following actions taken by businesspeople to make contacts in Korea or Egypt. Decide whether each action is a good idea. Write *Yes* for a good idea and *No* for a bad idea. Discuss your answers with the class.

South Korea

_____ a. A businesswoman preparing for her first business trip to South Korea writes up a personal biography describing her family background, education, and work history.

_____ b. She then goes directly to all of the businesses that interest her. She introduces herself and hands them her biography, along with information about her business.

Egypt

_____ a. In preparation for his first business trip to Egypt, a businessman from a small company contacts a member of U.S. Congress and gets a reference for his business. Then he contacts the Egyptian businesses.

_____ b. He meets the business contacts and spends many hours socializing with them and their friends. After they have developed a good social relationship, he begins to talk business.

| Introductions | There are many ways of introducing oneself, as the following South Korean-American encounter illustrates. |

| **A SOUTH KOREAN– AMERICAN ENCOUNTER** | An American executive working in South Korea said, "I learned about Korean handshaking customs my first day at work. I had just entered the bank in Seoul where I would have my office. When I was introduced to a female member of my new staff, I naturally extended my hand and shook her hand. She turned deep red. Everyone in the department laughed."[1] |

1 Neil Chesanow, *The World Class Executive*, New York: Rawson Associates, 1985.

In the United States, a man and a woman shake hands, as do two men or two women. Either the man or the woman can begin the handshake; often the person with more authority begins the handshake. The businessman in this minicase was acting as though he were in the United States by extending his hand to the Korean woman.

In South Korean introductions, two men shake hands and two women bow. But in an introduction between a man and a woman, one can bow or shake hands. If they shake hands, the woman always begins the handshake. She is giving the man permission to touch her hand. If a man begins the handshake, he is touching her without her permission. This causes embarrassment.

Your Point of View

In small groups of students from your country think about the introductions described below. Demonstrate these introductions to the class in your native language and afterward explain what was said.

a. Self-introduction to someone at a party (between two men; a man and a woman; and two women)
b. Self-introduction to a colleague at a business conference (between two men; a man and a woman; and two women)

Discussion

Watch the introductions and answer the following questions as a class.

1. How much touching is there in each introduction?
2. How much distance is there between the two people in each introduction?
3. What are some differences between the social and business introductions?
4. What are the differences among introductions involving two men, a man and a woman, and two women?

Names and Titles

There are many different traditions for addressing people in the world. In some cultures people use each other's first name immediately. In other cultures, the first name is only used by close friends and family. And in some cultures the first name is the family name and the second name is the given name.

A SINGAPOREAN–AMERICAN ENCOUNTER

A partner in one of New York's leading private banking firms went to Singapore to meet one of his clients. In Singapore there are three different cultural traditions: Chinese, Malaysian, and English. His clients were ethnic Chinese.

The banker wanted to do everything correctly, so on his way to Singapore he memorized the names of the three representatives he would meet. In the first meeting with the representatives and some other business contacts, he began by addressing the top man, Lo Win Hao, as Mr. Hao. As the meeting continued, he made sure to address each representative by name. After a while, one of the contacts passed a note to the American banker. The note said "Too friendly, too soon."[2]

Discussion

Answer the following questions in groups.

1. What did this note mean? What mistake was the banker making? (After you discuss your ideas, read the answer in Appendix Activity 3.)
2. Why is it important to know about the traditions for addressing your foreign business partners?
3. Have you ever been called by the wrong name or had your name pronounced incorrectly? How did you feel? What did you do? Did you correct the person or ignore the mistake?

---

[2] Lennie Copeland and Lewis Griggs, *Going International*, Random House, 1985.

Your Point of View

Answer the following questions about titles in your culture. Share your answers with a partner and compare them to those of an American provided in the chart.

	You	Your Classmate	One American's Response
1. How do you address classmates in your home country?			*By first name or nickname.*
2. How do you address your business colleagues in your home country?			*By first name or nickname.*
3. What different titles do you use for women?			*We use Miss or Ms. for unmarried women and Mrs. or Ms. for married women.*
4. What different titles do you use for men?			*We always use Mr. for both young and old, married and unmarried.*
5. How do you address a person at your business/social level if you have just met?			*Usually by first name.*
6. How do you address a boss or supervisor?			*Usually by first name. If there is a large difference in power, we may use Mr. or Ms.*
7. How do you address a secretary or receptionist?			*By first name.*
8. Are there special titles for people in a company depending on their position or their education? Do you use these titles?			*In a company we do not use different titles for different positions. Educators and other professionals sometimes use their academic titles but mainly in business cards and letters.*

LANGUAGE EXPANSION

Expressions and Idioms

There are many idioms in English that describe how a relationship develops. Match the idioms with their definitions.

_____ 1. to hit it off   a. to like someone immediately

_____ 2. to break the ice   b. to have a good relationship

_____ 3. to get along with   c. to get past the beginning of an introduction

_____ 4. to get to know

_____ 5. to warm up to   d. to begin to like a person

      e. to learn more about a person

Complete the following sentences with the correct idioms.

1. At first the employees were nervous about the new director. They thought she was too strict, but after a few months they realized she just wanted the best for the project and they _____ her.

2. I met a lot of people at the conference but I was too busy to _____ anyone very well. I hope this year I can follow up and meet with some of these contacts.

3. They met at a stockholders' meeting and _____. Within weeks, they were planning a new venture together.

4. The new head of sales does not _____ with his employees. This will have a bad effect on the whole department.

5. On the first day of the seminar the participants all had dinner together _____.

Word Forms

Often the same word base can be used in the verb, noun, and adjective forms. Some nouns and adjectives have more than one form. Complete the following chart with the missing forms.

Verb	Noun	Adjective
adapt		adaptable
contact		contacted
accustom (oneself)		customary
	impression	impressive
	information	informative
introduce		introductory
	reference	referred
		reputable

Complete the following sentences with the correct verb, noun, or adjective form of the words in the chart above. Use one form of each word base, and do not repeat any words.

1. She tried to _____ the sales representative, but he never returned her calls.

2. Before doing business in a foreign country, it is useful to learn some of the common business practices and _____.

3. The young executive wanted to _____ his colleagues, so he dressed his best.

4. We had never bought their products before, so the company gave us a special _____ price.

5. We employed him because he had excellent _____ from some top people in the field, but so far his work has not been good.

6. In order to dominate the market, the company now makes computer parts that are _____ to all models.

7. The meeting was useful because a lot of new _____ was presented.

8. It took him forty years to build his _____ and one night to destroy it. One mistake can cost a political career.

BIBLIOGRAPHY

Axtell, Roger F. *Do's and Taboos around the World*. New York: John Wiley & Sons, 1990.

Chesanow, Neil. *The World Class Executive*. New York: Rawson Associates, 1985.

Copeland, Lennie, and Lewis Griggs. *Going International*. New York: Random House, 1985.

de Mente, Boye. *Korean Etiquette and Ethics in Business*. Illinois: NTC Business Books, 1991.

Erdener, Kaynak. *International Business in the Middle East*. New York: Walter de Gruyter, 1986.

Zimmerman, Mark. *How to Do Business with the Japanese*. New York: Random House, 1985.

HOSPITALITY
ACROSS
CULTURES

Unit

1. Where are these people?
2. What are these people doing?
3. Are they friends or work colleagues? How do you know?
4. What is the purpose of having a party with work colleagues?

CASE STUDY

AN OFFICE PARTY

An American manager by the name of Bill Morris worked for an American multinational firm. One year he was transferred to France. When he began working in the French office, he wanted to get to know his employees and show them that he was friendly and interested in a good work relationship. He decided **to throw a party** for the whole office. He thought it would be a good way **to get acquainted with** everyone in a less **formal** environment. He invited everyone in his office, including secretaries and executives, for a big party in his elegant apartment. Everyone accepted the invitation. He was pleased that no one **had declined** his invitation.

At his apartment Morris served **a buffet** of snack foods and drinks. The employees could **help themselves to** whatever they liked. The manager liked this **casual** style of parties. As an informal and relaxed **host of the party** he could show them that he was an open person and easy to talk to. Morris feels these are important qualities of a manager and boss.

The party, however, was not a success. The employees were very uncomfortable as **guests**. They felt they didn't know Morris well enough to be in his home. They thought he was showing off his money by inviting them to his elegant apartment. They also were not comfortable with one another because they were not used to **socializing** together.

Vocabulary

Circle the words that are most similar in meaning to the words in italics (taken from the story).

1. He decided *to throw a party* for the whole office.
    a. to go out with a group of people
    b. to have a party
    c. to go to a party

2. He thought it would be a good way *to get acquainted with* everyone.
    a. to get to know
    b. to get tired of
    c. to please

3. He thought the workplace was too *formal* to get to know the employees well.
   a. relaxed
   b. impersonal
   c. busy

4. He was pleased that no one *had declined* his invitation.
   a. had said maybe to
   b. had said yes to
   c. had said no to

5. At the house he served *a buffet* of snack foods and drinks.
   a. a small amount
   b. a meal eaten around a table
   c. food to be eaten away from the table

6. The employees could *help themselves to* whatever they liked.
   a. help each other eat
   b. serve themselves
   c. do

7. The manager liked this *casual* style of parties.
   a. relaxed
   b. impersonal
   c. happy

8. As an informal *host of the party* he could show them that he was an open person and easy to talk to.
   a. person who gives a party
   b. person who goes to a party
   c. person who makes jokes at a party

9. The employees were very uncomfortable as *guests* in his home.
   a. servants
   b. friends
   c. invited people

10. They also were not used to *socializing* together.
    a. spending time together while working
    b. spending time together as friends
    c. spending time together while eating

Reviewing the Case

Answer the following questions and share your answers with a partner.

1. Why did Bill Morris decide to throw the party?
2. Why did Morris want his party to be casual?
3. According to Morris what are good social qualities of a manager and boss?
4. Why were the employees uncomfortable at Morris's party?

Making Inferences

Read the following list of expectations. Put an *M* next to those of Bill Morris and an *E* next to those of the employees. The first one is done for you. Share your answers with a partner.

_____*E*_____ 1. A manager should be formal with his employees.

_____ 2. Work relationships and social relationships are separate.

_____ 3. A good work environment develops from good social relationships at the workplace.

_____ 4. A manager should be an easy person to relate to.

_____ 5. A manager should show a clear sense of authority.

_____ 6. Home is a private place for family and close friends.

_____ 7. Inviting people to one's home is a sign of generosity and hospitality.

_____ 8. All the employees in the office should feel like one big family.

_____ 9. A manager should be able to socialize with any employee in his or her office.

_____ 10. Inviting business colleagues one hardly knows to one's home is just showing off.

Problem Solving: Information Gap

The company which sent the manager to France has heard that things aren't going well in the Paris office. You are to investigate the different cultural backgrounds of the manager and the employees. Then you will develop a solution.

Divide the class into two groups: A and B. Group A reads the French cultural information in Appendix Activity 22. Group B reads the American cultural information in Appendix Activity 24. After reading the information, complete your part of the chart below. Next, find a partner from the other group and ask questions to complete the chart.

	In France	In the United States
1. Is it common to socialize with employees from different levels of the company?		
2. What is the role of the boss in the social life of the office?		
3. Is the style of entertaining colleagues formal or informal?		
4. Is it common to entertain business colleagues at home? Why or why not?		
5. What is different about socializing with friends and socializing with colleagues?		
6. What are common ways of socializing with business colleagues?		

Discussion

Go back to your groups. Look at the completed chart and discuss the following questions.

1. Now that you have more information about both cultures, do you want to change any of your answers from Making Inferences on page 35? Discuss your changes if any.
2. What difference in the U.S. and French office cultures had the most serious effect on the relationship between the manager and his employees?

Written Reflection

This case is about a manager in a U.S. multinational corporation. The organization of the corporation and its work culture are American, not French. Headquarters does, however, allow local managers to adapt to local social culture if it seems appropriate. Do you think Bill Morris should adapt to the social ways of his French employees? How much should the French employees adapt, considering they work for a U.S. corporation?

Write out a plan for Bill Morris and his employees that compromises between their two office cultures. Make sure the plan helps develop good employee relations and high office morale. To help you organize your plan, review the points in the chart. When you are finished, share your plan with the class.

AROUND THE WORLD

Socializing with Colleagues

As you learned in the above case, different cultures have different ideas about socializing with colleagues. In some cultures, office colleagues often go out to eat and drink with one another. In other cultures, only friends go out together, and work relationships are more distant and formal.

Your Point of View

Check the places you go and things you do with friends. Then check the places you go and things you do with colleagues.

WITH FRIENDS	WITH COLLEAGUES
Where to Go	**Where to Go**
_____ Bar	_____ Bar
_____ Restaurant	_____ Restaurant
_____ Night club	_____ Night club
_____ Home	_____ Home
_____ Country house	_____ Country house
_____ Golf or tennis club	_____ Golf or tennis club
_____ Beach or mountains	_____ Beach or mountains
_____ Bath house or hot springs	_____ Bath house or hot springs
_____ Other: _____	_____ Other: _____
What to Do	**What to Do**
_____ Drink together	_____ Drink together
_____ Go out for breakfast	_____ Go out for breakfast
_____ Go out to lunch	_____ Go out to lunch
_____ Go out to dinner	_____ Go out to dinner
_____ Throw a party	_____ Throw a party
_____ Go dancing	_____ Go dancing
_____ Have a banquet	_____ Have a banquet
_____ Play a sport together	_____ Play a sport together
_____ Go to a cultural or sports event	_____ Go to a cultural or sports event
_____ Get together with family	_____ Get together with family
_____ Other: _____	_____ Other: _____

Discussion

Answer the following questions as a class.

1. What is different about the social time you spend with friends and the social time you spend with colleagues?
2. How often do you go out with colleagues?
3. Do you think it is good to socialize with your colleagues? Why or why not?
4. In English there is a saying, "Never mix business with pleasure." Do you agree with this saying? Why or why not?

Entertaining Business Clients

Cultures also differ when it comes to entertaining business clients.

Read the following examples and then say what is done in your culture.

South Korea	Dinner parties, drinking, and singing in Karaoke bars and sometimes in *ksaengs* (nightclubs with hostesses). Playing golf together. Spouses are not usually included.
Spain	Usually lunch or dinner in a restaurant, not someone's home. Spouses rarely come along. Guests may be accompanied or offered tickets to cultural events.
United States	Dinner in a restaurant or at home. Spouses are often included. Playing golf, tennis, or racquetball. Guests may be accompanied or offered tickets to cultural or sports events.
Your country	

Your Point of View

You work for the Chamber of Commerce (a local association that invites and encourages business). Several representatives of a large entertainment company from the United States are coming to your city. The company is interested in building an amusement park in the area. This would be a great tourist benefit to your city. You want to welcome the company's representatives and see that they are well entertained on their two-day visit. There are three men and one woman in the group. They are all in their early fifties and are all top-level executives. The group will arrive Tuesday afternoon after a five-hour flight and will leave Thursday at 5:00 P.M. Approximately six hours each day will be spent talking about business.

Plan a two-day hospitality agenda for the group to present to the class. Before writing your plan, consider the following questions.

1. What special parts of your city would you like the representatives to visit?
2. Considering their work, what would they be most interested in seeing?
3. How could you make them feel most welcome?

Discussion

Answer the following questions as a class.

1. Which agendas were most interesting? Why?
2. Which agendas do you think were most appropriate for this group of visitors? Why?
3. Which agenda considered the cultural hospitality style of Americans? Do you think the cultural hospitality style of the visitors should be considered in an agenda? Why or why not?

Gift Giving

There are many ways of giving and accepting gifts, as this Saudi-German encounter illustrates.

A Saudi–German Encounter

Bouchaib Alsadoun, a Saudi businessman, invited Johann Wuerth, a German businessman, to dinner at his house. Johann entered the elegant house and offered his gift of a bottle of Scotch whiskey and a box of butter cookies to his host. Bouchaib was embarrassed by the gifts and quickly put them away. They then sat down in the living room area. Bouchaib offered Johann a cup of coffee, which he quickly accepted. Bouchaib thought his guest was a bit rude. As they drank coffee Johann complimented Bouchaib on an art book on the living room table. The Saudi businessman responded by offering him the book. Johann, embarrassed, said, "No thank you! It is very kind of you, but I can't accept it!" Bouchaib was offended by his guest's behavior. Although Johann sensed this, he couldn't imagine how he had offended Bouchaib.

Discussion

Answer the following questions as a class.

1. What three actions offended Bouchaib? Why do you think these offended him? (After you discuss this, read Appendix Activity 10 for the answer.)
2. What can Johann do now that he has offended his host?
3. Can a misunderstanding like this one really affect the business relationship? If so, how?

Your Point of View

Answer the following questions about gift giving in your culture. Share your answers with a classmate, if possible someone from another culture. Also compare your answers to those of an American as listed in the chart.

	You	Your Classmate	One American's Response
1. On what occasions do you give gifts to business colleagues? (on birthdays? for the New Year?)			Usually on birthdays, for weddings, and sometimes at Christmas time.
2. What kinds of gifts might you expect from colleagues? (liquor, pens, books, other?) Would expensive gifts be appropriate?			Pens, books, plants, compact disks, or gift-certificates. Gifts over the value of $50 are not appropriate.
3. How should a person respond when given a gift? Should the person open the gift in front of the giver or wait to open the gift when alone?			The person should open the gift in front of the giver.
4. How do you thank someone for a gift?			I tell the person how much I like the gift when I open it. I then follow up with a short written note thanking the person again.
5. On the same occasion what is the difference between an employee's gift to a supervisor and a supervisor's gift to an employee? Who gives the bigger gift? Why?			Employees usually give group gifts to their supervisor so that the gift is not perceived as a special favor from any one employee. The supervisor gives small gifts to employees, but never of significant value.

Discussion

Answer the following questions as a class.

1. According to the chart, what are some similarities of gift-giving practices across cultures?
2. According to the chart, where could misunderstandings develop between businesspeople when giving gifts?
3. Have you ever received an embarrassing gift? What was it? Why was it embarrassing? How did you respond?
4. Do you like to give gifts? In the United States there is a saying, "It is better to give than to receive." Do you agree with this saying?

LANGUAGE EXPANSION

Expressions and Idioms

There are many different idioms in English for talking about hospitality and entertaining. Match the expressions with their definitions.

_____ 1. to go out on the town

_____ 2. to wine and dine (someone)

_____ 3. a token of (one's) appreciation

_____ 4. it (the bill) is on us

_____ 5. to take (someone) out to

a. a small gift or gesture that expresses thanks

b. to go out at night and visit many different places

c. to invite someone to something

d. to try to impress someone with good food and drink

e. we will pay

Complete the following sentences with the correct expressions.

1. When the waiter brought the bill, the businesswoman said to her client, "No. Don't worry about it. _____."

2. When the team came from Singapore, they expressed interest in seeing the sights of the city. So, with the host company, they _____ .They saw a show, went to a bar, and had dinner in the best restaurant in town.

3. In an attempt to get the account, the young businessman _____ the purchaser at an elegant restaurant. They had a wonderful time, but the purchaser didn't give him the account.

4. They planned an interesting agenda for the visiting partners. First they _____ them _____ the tennis club for lunch, and then they toured downtown.

5. A couple of days after the visit, the host company received a small gift as _____ for the visit.

Word Forms

Often the same word base can be used in verb, noun, and adjective forms. Complete the following chart with the missing forms.

Verb	Noun	Adjective
	acceptance	acceptable
get acquainted with		acquainted
appreciate		appreciative
compliment		complimentary
entertain		entertaining
		hospitable
invite		invited
	socializing	social

Complete each sentence with the correct verb, noun, or adjective form of the words in the chart above. Use one form of each word base once, and do not repeat any words.

1. There are many ways to express _____ in the United States. One way is to send a thank-you note.

2. In South Korea businesspeople often _____ new colleagues by going to restaurants to eat and drink together.

3. In China if one receives a(n)_____ , one should not say, "Thank you."

4. In the United States it is common to receive a(n) _____ to dinner at a person's home.

5. _____ with colleagues after business hours is an important part of work life in Japan.

6. Every culture has different ideas of what is appropriate behavior. In the United States businesspeople sometimes put their feet up on a desk. In Arab cultures this is not _____ behavior. There, the bottom of the foot is considered dirty and should not be shown to anyone.

7. In the United States, a common way to _____ is to throw a party.

8. Middle Eastern countries are known for their great tradition of _____ .

BIBLIOGRAPHY

Axtell, Roger F. *Do's and Taboos around the World.* New York: John Wiley and Sons, 1990.

Axtell, Roger F. *Do's and Taboos of Hosting International Visitors.* New York: John Wiley and Sons, 1990.

Chesanow, Neil. *The World Class Executive.* New York: Rawson Associates, 1985.

Copeland, Lennie, and Lewis Griggs. *Going International.* New York: Random House, 1985.

de Mente, Boye. *Chinese Etiquette and Ethics in Business.* Illinois: NTC Business Books, 1990.

de Mente, Boye. *Korean Etiquette and Ethics in Business.* Illinois: NTC Business Books, 1991.

Lee, O. Young, and Seong-Kon Kim. *Simple Etiquette in Korea.* England: Paul Norbury Publications, 1988.

Leppert, Paul A. *How to Do Business with Chinese.* San Diego, CA: Patton Pacific Press, 1984.

TIME ACROSS
CULTURES

Unit 4

"Timing is Everything."

Cartoon courtesy of Harvard Business Review, 1988.

1. In the United States, the expression "timing is everything" means that the most important factor to success is often not what is done, but when something is done. Do you agree with this expression? Why or why not?

2. Are you careful about how you use time? Do you try to make schedules for yourself? Do you stick to them?

3. Are you concerned about getting to class, work, or appointments on time? (On time means exactly at the arranged time.) In your culture, how important is it to be on time and not late for appointments and meetings?

CASE STUDY

ITALIAN – SWISS BREAKDOWN

A major Italian manufacturing company needed a new computerized system for its **shipping and handling** department. The Italian company **hired** a Swiss software and engineering company to develop the computerized equipment. This equipment was going to be put in the Italian company's **warehouses**.

The two companies agreed on a plan with the following four **phases**: 1) develop software **specifications** for the shipping and handling department, 2) design the software, 3) make the computerized machines using the software, and 4) put the new equipment in the warehouses. They also developed a general **schedule** of when each phase should be completed.

In the first phase, the two companies agreed on the **preliminary** specifications for the new software and began to write a more detailed description of these specifications. At first, these meetings were friendly and effective. The two teams used English in the meetings and had no difficulty speaking to each other. However, within three months there was a **breakdown** in communication and cooperation between the two companies.

The Swiss engineers complained that the Italian team changed the software plans too frequently. Every time the Swiss team thought they had an agreement on the detailed specifications of the computer software, the Italian team came up with new ideas and changes which **delayed** the project. The Swiss team complained that the Italians were often late and therefore the **deadlines** were not being met.

The Italian team also had complaints. They said that after the preliminary specifications were made, they thought of some basic ideas that would lead to great improvements. The Swiss team rejected the new ideas even though the new ideas might be important because they said they were finished with that step in the process. The Italian team complained that the Swiss team required **fixed** dates for everything and only cared about keeping the schedule.

Vocabulary

Match the following words (taken from the story) to their definitions.

____ 1. shipping and handling

____ 2. hire

____ 3. warehouse

____ 4. phase

____ 5. specification

____ 6. schedule

____ 7. preliminary

____ 8. breakdown

____ 9. delay

____ 10. deadline

____ 11. fixed

a. failure

b. not able to be moved; not flexible

c. something that comes first with other things following

d. slow down something in progress

e. detail or aspect of a plan

f. step or stage

g. a date or time before which something must be done

h. storing, packing, and sending goods

i. place to store goods

j. timetable or plan of time for doing things

k. employ

Reviewing the Case

Answer the following questions and share your answers with a partner.

1. Why did the Italian manufacturing company hire the Swiss engineering company?
2. How many phases did the plan have that the companies agreed on? In what phase would they decide on the Italian company's software needs?
3. Was language a problem in their meetings?
4. What were some of the problems the two teams had with each other? Complete the following chart.

	Italian Team Says	Swiss Team Says
Plans		*Italian team always changes plans after agreed time*
Deadlines		
Schedules		

Making Inferences

Answer the following questions and share your answers with a partner.

1. Why do you think the Italian team often changed their software plans?
2. Why do you think the Italian team missed the deadlines?
3. Why do you think the Swiss team refused the Italian team's new ideas?
4. Why do you think the Swiss team required fixed deadlines?

Problem Solving: Information Gap

The Italian and the Swiss teams have asked you and your classmates to help them with their time management problems. You will read information about these cultures that will help you with your solutions.

Divide the class into two groups: A and B. Group A reads the Italian cultural information in Appendix Activity 18. Group B reads the Swiss cultural information in Appendix Activity 28. After reading the information, complete your part of the following chart. Next, find a partner from the other group and ask questions to complete the chart.

	In Italy	In Switzerland
1. Is it usual to work on several phases of a project at the same time?		
2. Is it important to measure time carefully? Why or why not?		
3. Should a schedule be flexible? Why or why not?		
4. Is a broken deadline a problem? Why or why not?		

Discussion

Go back to your groups, look at the completed chart, and discuss the following.

1. Now that you have more information about both cultures, do you want to change any of your answers from Making Inferences on page 51? Discuss your changes if any.
2. What difference between the two teams has the most serious effect on this project?
3. The following are four possible solutions. Which of the four do you like best? Or, come up with a solution of your own. Consider the following issues as you make your decision:
   - quality of product
   - financial cost of the solution
   - amount of time needed for the solution
   - further international business opportunities
   - feasibility (is it really possible?)

What are the positive and negative consequences of each solution? Why is the solution you have chosen the best? Discuss your answers in groups.

   a. The Italian company decided that it would be easier to have another Italian company complete the project rather than continue to work with the Swiss company. It found an Italian software and engineering company whose credentials were good although not as good as those of the Swiss software company.

   b. The Italian company agreed to never modify the plans and to meet all deadlines. In other words, they would adopt the Swiss company's business practices.

   c. The Italian and Swiss teams decided to live for a short period of time in each other's countries. In this way they could learn to appreciate the time value differences in each country and learn more about each other's cultures.

   d. The Swiss company agreed to forget the deadlines and be more flexible with the original specifications. In other words they would adopt the Italian company's business practices.

   e. Your own solution.

4. Read the actual solution in Appendix Activity 12. Why do you think the companies chose this solution? Do you think a short period of time is enough to gain an understanding of a foreign culture?

Written Reflection

In the actual solution to the case the two companies planned to continue working together once they had learned about each other's time management styles. To what extent do you think the two companies had to adapt to each other's cultures?

Write up a time management plan for the companies to follow when working together. Your plan must include compromises between the Italian and Swiss time management styles. To help you organize your plan, review the issues in the chart above. When you have finished, share your plan with the class.

AROUND THE WORLD

Punctuality   When businesspeople from different time orientations (monochronic and polychronic) do business together, problems can occur, especially with punctuality, since monochronic cultures depend much more on fixed schedules than do polychronic cultures. *Punctuality* means that when you set a time for an appointment or a date, you arrive exactly at the time set and no later.

Your Point of View

In your point of view, what is the appropriate time to arrive for the following events?   Share your answers as a class.

Event	Arrival Time
a. A doctor's appointment for 8:30 A.M.	
b. A class that begins at 2:00 P.M.	
c. A business meeting set for 3:30 P.M.	
d. Your job that starts 9:00 A.M.	
e. A train that is scheduled to leave at 7:17 P.M.	
f. A dinner party at a friend's house set for 6:30 P.M.	

Discussion

Compare your answers from *Your Point of View* with those of an American in Appendix Activity 6. Answer the following questions as a class.

1. How do your answers differ from the other students' and the American's answers?
2. For the events above, how late would you have to be before you would have to apologize?
3. What do your answers tell you about your culture and punctuality? Do you think you are from a generally monochronic or polychronic culture? Based on what you know and on the American's responses, do you think the United States is a monochronic or polychronic culture?

4. Imagine you are going to do business with a person from a different time orientation than yours. How would you react to the differences? How would you prepare yourself for the differences in punctuality and schedules?

5. The following are some more examples of countries whose cultures tend to be monochronic or polychronic. Enter your country and as many other countries as you know about in the spaces provided.

MONOCHRONIC	POLYCHRONIC
United States	Greece
Canada	Portugal
Australia	France
Sweden	Spain
Norway	Brazil
Denmark	Colombia
Germany	Mexico
Austria	Nigeria
_____	_____
_____	_____
_____	_____
_____	_____
_____	_____
_____	_____
_____	_____
_____	_____
_____	_____
_____	_____
_____	_____
_____	_____
_____	_____
_____	_____
_____	_____
_____	_____

Business Schedules Most companies have daily and weekly work schedules that determine when the company is open and closed, when the employees have lunch, and when the employees can take breaks. These schedules vary within countries, but there are general work times that may apply to many companies within one culture. The following schedules are typical workday schedules of small businesses in several cities around the world.

Read the three completed schedules, and then complete the schedule for a business in your hometown.

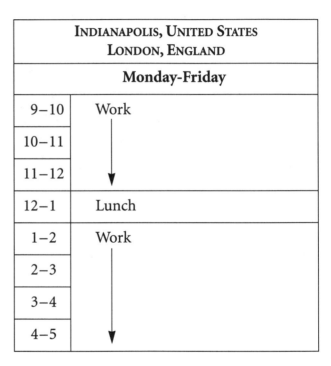

INDIANAPOLIS, UNITED STATES LONDON, ENGLAND	
Monday–Friday	
9–10	Work
10–11	
11–12	
12–1	Lunch
1–2	Work
2–3	
3–4	
4–5	

VERONA, ITALY	
Monday–Friday	
9–10	Work
10–11	
11–12	
12–1	
1–2	
2–3	
3–4	Lunch
4–5	
5–6	Work
6–7	
7–8	

KUWAIT CITY, KUWAIT	
Saturday–Thursday	
8 – 9	Work
9 – 10	
10 – 11	
11 – 12	
12 – 1	
1 – 2	Lunch
2 – 3	
3 – 4	Work
4 – 5	
5 – 6	
6 – 7	
7 – 8	

(Work stops for prayer five times a day.)

A BUSINESS IN YOUR HOMETOWN	
8 – 9	
9 – 10	
10 – 11	
11 – 12	
12 – 1	
1 – 2	
2 – 3	
3 – 4	
4 – 5	
5 – 6	
6 – 7	
7 – 8	

Discussion

Answer the following questions as a class.

1. Identify three differences among the schedules including your own. Can you explain some of the reasons for the differences in these schedules?
2. In your country, do business places such as those selling clothing and food have the same schedules as business offices? If not, how are they different?
3. In businesses in your country, do you have to have breaks? In what kind of businesses? When are the breaks and how long are they? What do you do during breaks?
4. What kind of schedule do you personally prefer? Why?
5. In what ways do different work schedules affect business communication (telephone and fax) between international companies? Imagine that the Italian company and the British company above agree to work on a project. After two months, the two companies begin to have problems communicating with each other. The British company cannot get in touch with the Italian company in the afternoon hours when they most need to communicate. The Italian company cannot get in touch with the British company during the evening hours when they need to communicate. What are some solutions to this communication problem?

Company Time or Personal Time

One more way to look at time is to divide it into two categories: company time and personal time. *Company time* is the time you spend at work or doing work-related activities, such as reviewing a report at home or going to an office cocktail party in the evening to socialize with co-workers. It is the time given to the good of the company. *Personal time* is the time you spend with family or friends. It is the time you have to yourself.

Every culture and individual balances these two types of time differently. In some cultures, company time is often more valued than personal time. This means that when life gets busy, personal time will be sacrificed for company needs. In many other cultures, personal time can take priority and company time may be sacrificed to meet the needs of friends and family.

Your Point of View

Read the following two situations and decide what you would do in each. Share your decisions with the class. Explain your decisions. If you decided to sacrifice personal time in one situation but company time in the other, explain the reasons for your decisions.

Situation 1:

Ms. Larden has planned a short weekend trip to her hometown to attend her parents' fiftieth wedding anniversary. Friday afternoon at four o'clock, just one hour before she had planned to leave, her boss informs her that he needs a report by 8:00 A.M. on Monday. She knows that a prompt and well-written report will greatly increase her possibility of getting the promotion she has been seeking. To get the report finished by Monday morning, Ms. Larden would have to spend the whole weekend in the office.

Situation 2:

Mr. Olsen is a manager of sales in an automobile company. This evening is his twenty-first wedding anniversary. He had planned to go out to dinner with his wife to celebrate. It is four o'clock and he has just learned that a group of new clients are in town and would like to go out with him in the evening. This is the only night they will be in town, and their business is important to Mr. Olsen.

Discussion

Answer the following questions as a class.

1. Are you working now? How many hours a week do you work?
2. How many hours a week does a businessperson usually work in your country? Is that too much time, too little time, or just about right? Why?
3. How much vacation time does a businessperson usually get in your country? Is that too much vacation, too little, or just about right? Why?
4. Would you ever bring work home with you from the office? Under what circumstances?
5. In your opinion, what kind of jobs require more company time? What jobs require minimal company time?
6. What percentage of a seven-day week do you dedicate to company time?
7. What is more important to you, company time or personal time? Why?

LANGUAGE EXPANSION

Expressions and Idioms

In the United States, the proverb "time is money" is commonly used. Time is spoken about as if it were money. According to U.S. idioms, one can budget, lose, save, invest, give, and spend time.

> to budget time
> to lose time on
> to save time
> to invest time in
> to give time
> to spend time on

Complete the following sentences with the correct idiom.

1. The busy manager needs to _____ his time more carefully. Today he missed two important meetings because his schedule was so badly organized.

2. We are _____ time on this deal. They will never agree to sign the contract. We should begin to move on to something else.

3. Don't leave now! Think of all the time you _____ in this project!

4. Excuse me, could you _____ me a minute of your time? I just have one small question.

5. You _____ too much time on the project this week. All your other work is past deadline.

6. In order to _____ time, the company decided to use computers in the purchasing department. The handwritten forms took too long to complete.

Word Forms

Often the same word base can be used in verb, noun, and adjective forms. Complete the following chart with the missing forms.

Verb	Noun	Adjective
schedule		scheduled
	modification	modified
		punctual
	prediction	predictable
measure	measurement	
	warehouse	
	specification	specific
communicate		communicative

Complete the following sentences with the correct verb, noun, or adjective form of the words in the chart above. Use one form of each word base, and do not repeat any words.

1. The main office_____ had to be taken into consideration during planning otherwise the computerized machinery might not have fit.

2. _____ is extremely important to many people. If you are late, they become insulted.

3. The company_____ were located five kilometers away from the main offices. Without computers, this made it hard to see exactly what products they had in storage.

4. We are_____ too many interviews on Tuesday morning. By the fifth one, we will all be exhausted.

5. By the end of the project_____ between the two companies was so good that there were no more time management problems and everyone understood each other.

6. Everything seemed to work so well between the two companies in the beginning that it was impossible _____ all the problems that they had by the second phase of the project.

7. The Italian team_____ exactly what they wanted the new machines to do. This made it easier for the Swiss team to design the computer software.

8. The _____ plans were much more successful than the previous ones. The changes were perfect.

BIBLIOGRAPHY

Brown, Robert. "Swatch vs. the Sundial: A Study in Different Attitudes towards Time," *International Management,* December 1987: p.80.

Moran, Robert T., and William G. Stripp. *Dynamics of Successful Business Interactions.* Houston: Gulf Publishing, 1991.

Terpstra, Vern, and Kenneth David. *The Cultural Environment of International Business.* Cincinnati, Ohio: South-Western Publishing, 1991.

Victor, David A. *International Business Communication.* New York: HarperCollins, 1992.

DECISION MAKERS ACROSS CULTURES

Unit 5

1. Who is the visiting businessperson in the picture? How can you tell?
2. How do you think he or she feels?
3. What signals is he or she giving to the other negotiators?
4. How can knowing about the following aspects of the other culture help you when preparing to do business overseas?
   - characteristics of typical negotiators from the other country (age, sex, social level, educational level)
   - tendency to negotiate in teams or alone
5. Have you ever lived in another country? If yes, were you ever in a situation where you felt culturally unprepared? In other words, did you ever feel like you did something inappropriate because you did not know about the culture? Share your stories.

WHOM SHOULD WE SEND?

A U.S.-based computer software company has recently heard from a Nigerian manufacturing company. The Nigerian company has expressed interest in one of its software programs. The Nigerian company has invited the U.S. company to Nigeria to **demonstrate** its software.

The U.S. company has been very successful **domestically**, but this will be the first time it has ever **ventured** into the international business world. The company would like to expand and begin to build **status** in the international community. Being successful with this negotiation would help the company very much.

The top managers have come together to plan a business **strategy** for the Nigerian business trip. They must also decide who is the most appropriate person to send to Nigeria to represent the company. The person chosen must be a highly **competent** negotiator, able to **persuade** the Nigerians that the company's software is the best in the market and exactly what the Nigerian company needs. Therefore, they must think very carefully about the **qualities** of the person they send.

Vocabulary

Match the following words (taken from the story) to their definitions.

_____ 1. demonstrate	a. plan
_____ 2. domestically	b. advance with risk
_____ 3. venture	c. position
_____ 4. status	d. capable, skilled
_____ 5. strategy	e. explain or show
_____ 6. competent	f. nationally or in the home country
_____ 7. persuade	g. convince
_____ 8. qualities	h. characteristics or features

Reviewing the Case

Answer the following questions and share your answers with a partner.

1. What does the Nigerian company want the U.S. company to do?
2. Why is it so important for the U.S. company to get a contract with the Nigerian company?
3. What must the U.S. negotiator be able to do in Nigeria?

Making Inferences

Answer the following questions and share your answers in groups.

1. The following qualities can affect a negotiator's ability to negotiate successfully. Which qualities would you think are most important for the negotiator the U.S. company sends to Nigeria? Which qualities are least important? For each quality, circle the number that reflects how you feel.

NOTE: 1 = Very important 5 = Not important					
1. Educational background (degrees, universities attended)	1	2	3	4	5
2. Sex (male/female)	1	2	3	4	5
3. Age	1	2	3	4	5
4. Technical knowledge of the company's products	1	2	3	4	5
5. Seniority and experience in the company	1	2	3	4	5
6. Personal connections	1	2	3	4	5
7. Social competence, good social skills	1	2	3	4	5
8. Social status in the community	1	2	3	4	5
9. Power and authority position within the company (power to make decisions)	1	2	3	4	5
10. Symbolic position of authority within the company (no power to make decisions)	1	2	3	4	5
11. Respect for authority and rules	1	2	3	4	5

2. Read the following descriptions of three possible people the company could send to Nigeria. Discuss who you should send and who you should not send. What are the advantages and disadvantages of each person?

BOB DRISDALE: He has been working for the company for twenty years. He is fifty-five years old. He has seniority and company respect. He does not have technical knowledge of the software. He is in the upper-level management of the company and has the authority to make decisions. He knows company policy and the history of the company. He has very good social skills.

CHRISTINE HALE: She has been working at the company for five years. She is the manager of the software division. She has some technical knowledge of the software because she has been working with the project from the start. She graduated from Harvard University with a degree in computer science. She is very social and well mannered. She is thirty-two years old and she has authority to make decisions.

TED CONWAY: He is a new employee who has been working for the company for two years. He is twenty-five years old, energetic, and very ambitious. He knows the software better than anyone in the company because he created the software. He is able to answer any technical question about the software. He is not very social and some people find him quite cold and distant. He does not always follow company rules, as he feels they sometimes stop him from being creative.

3. Who is your final choice? Why? Which of the negotiator qualities from the chart does your choice have?

4. Would you consider sending a second person? Why or why not?

5. Do you think you should consider the characteristics of the other country's negotiators when deciding whom to send? Why or why not?

Problem Solving: Information Gap

You are going to read information about negotiators in Nigeria and in the United States. This information may help you further with your decision of whom to send.

Divide the class into two groups: A and B. Group A reads the Nigerian cultural information in Appendix Activity 21. Group B reads the U.S. cultural information in Appendix Activity 23. After reading the information, complete your part of the chart below. Next, find a partner from the other group and ask questions to complete the chart.

	In Nigeria	In the United States
1. If you are seriously interested in doing business, what qualities are most important in the negotiator you send? Why?		
2. How important is age?		
3. What gives a person respect in a company?		
4. What other qualities are important in a negotiator? What qualities are not important?		
5. What is the role of women in business?		
6. What is more common, negotiating in groups or alone?		

Discussion

Go back to your groups, look at the completed chart, and answer the following.

1. Which cultural differences could cause the most serious problems between the Nigerian and U.S. negotiators?
2. Based on the chart, what person or people do you think would be most appropriate to send to Nigeria? Does this choice differ from your group's initial choice?
3. Who would be the least appropriate person to send? Why?

Written Reflection

Imagine that you decided to send Ted Conway alone to Nigeria. What do you think would have happened? What reaction would Ted Conway have had? What reaction would the Nigerian team have had? What could they have done to rectify the situation and continue with negotiations?

Write one paragraph describing the problems that would have occurred and another paragraph discussing what could have been done to resolve the problem. To help you organize your plan, review the issues in the above chart. When you have finished, share your paragraphs with the class.

AROUND THE WORLD

Negotiator Qualities

Whom you send to negotiate a deal could actually make or break the deal. In some countries people with personal and social connections will be able to get in the door faster than people with no connections. In other countries, people with extensive technical knowledge will make a greater impression on the other team than those with personal connections. In almost all countries, negotiating in teams is more common than negotiating with only one person. Even the United States is turning more to team negotiating as U.S. companies realize its advantages.

Read the following information about negotiators around the world. Check the qualities you think are most important for a negotiator to have in order to negotiate successfully in your country and your classmate's country. Share your information with your classmates.

NEGOTIATOR QUALITIES FROM AROUND THE WORLD

	United States	Japan	Mexico	Brazil	France
Educational Background		✓	✓	✓	✓
Sex (male/ female negotiator)	male or female	mostly male	INA*	INA*	mostly male
Age		✓			
Technical Knowledge	✓	✓	✓		
Seniority/ Experience		✓	✓		
Power and Authority	✓				
Symbolic Position of Authority		✓			
Follows Standards					✓
Personal Connections			✓	✓	
Social Competence			✓	✓	✓
Social Status				✓	✓

*INA = information not available

Discussion

Answer the following questions as a class.

1. What information in the chart surprises you most?
2. Are you familiar with these countries? If so, do you agree with the information in the chart? Do you have any additional information?

NEGOTIATOR QUALITIES FROM AROUND THE WORLD, continued

	Germany	South Korea	Spain	Your Country	Your Classmate's
Educational Background		✓	✓		
Sex (male/ female negotiator)	mostly male	mostly male	mostly male		
Age	✓				
Technical Knowledge	✓	✓			
Seniority/ Experience	✓				
Power and Authority					
Symbolic Position of Authority					
Follows Standards					
Personal Connections			✓		
Social Competence					
Social Status		✓	✓		

3. Which country would you have the least problems negotiating with? Why? Which country would you have the most problems with? Why?

4. How would information like that in the chart affect your decision of whom to choose to negotiate for your company? Give an example.

5. In general, do you think countries are changing in what they consider important in a negotiator? If so, what is changing?

Styles of Persuasion

In addition to the characteristics discussed above, a person's persuasive style is also very important when negotiating. There are many different and successful ways to persuade someone to agree to something. In each culture there may be a common style of persuasion, but styles vary greatly from person to person. For example, in the United States, many people believe a persuasive negotiator should be competitive, direct, impersonal, and logical, but some Americans prefer a more yielding and indirect style. The success of a persuasion style also depends on the person who is being persuaded.

Your Point of View

The following are examples of two very different styles of persuasion. Each style has seven specific characteristics. Check the characteristics you find are most persuasive and state why. You can choose characteristics from both styles. Compare your answers in groups.

PERSUASIVE STYLE 1	PERSUASIVE STYLE 2
____ Being cooperative	____ Being competitive
____ Speaking indirectly so that no one is humiliated	____ Speaking directly
____ Making concessions	____ Not making concessions
____ Using emotion	____ Using logic
____ Being personal	____ Being impersonal
____ Not taking advantage of the other's weaknesses	____ Taking advantage of the other's weaknesses
____ Reacting slowly and carefully	____ Reacting quickly and decisively

Discussion

1. Are there characteristics that you all agree are generally most persuasive? If so, which?
2. Are there characteristics that you all agree are generally least persuasive? If so, which?
3. What differences of opinions are there in your groups? Do you think these differences are personal or cultural?
4. Under what circumstances would a negotiator need to change his or her style? Explain your answer.
5. Do you think negotiator styles are or should be different among men and women? Explain your answer.

Women and the Workplace

The role of women in the workplace is changing every year. In many countries such as the United States, women are entering occupations that were traditionally filled only by men and are becoming more visible at the managerial and decision-making levels. Many other countries, however, remain male dominated and not receptive to the presence of women in such positions. Although the business world is changing, some experts still advise against sending a woman as a negotiator to countries not receptive to women decision makers. If a woman is sent to such a country, they say she should go as a member of a team. Therefore, sending a woman who is successful in her home country to negotiate overseas is not always a simple or easy decision.

The following story describes one female K-Mart executive's successful experience negotiating in Saudi Arabia, a country known for not accepting women in its business world.

A SAUDI ARABIAN–AMERICAN ENCOUNTER

I went with another gentleman of our company who has a lesser position than I do. We met with a group of Saudis who epitomized the feelings of men in that country toward women. We were in the office of the chairman of the Saudi firm, and for the first hour he continually addressed my associate, ignoring me, because he would not accept my presence as a woman. Finally I turned to him and said: "Mr. X, you are directing your questions and answers to my associate. If you are seriously interested in doing business with our company, I suggest you direct them to me, because it is me with whom you will have to negotiate." I think he respected my approach. I didn't feel indignant or slighted as a woman. It was a matter of who it is that a person wants to seek out. I had no problems after that.[1]

[1]Neil Chesanow, *The World Class Executive*, New York: Rawson Associates, 1985.

Discussion

Answer the following questions in groups.

1. Why do you think the woman spoke as she did to the chairman? What persuasive style did she use and why?
2. Once she spoke, why do you think the chairman responded to her as he did?
3. Do you think all Saudi chairmen would have responded to her style in the same way? Explain your answer.
4. Would a foreign woman negotiating in your country be successful with a negotiating style like the one in the story? Would a national? Why or why not?
5. In your country, are foreign businesswomen treated differently from national businesswomen? If so, how?
6. What advice would you give to a foreign businesswoman in a similar position sent to your country to negotiate?

Applying Your Knowledge

Answer the following questions and share your answers in groups.

1. Are the following jobs typically held by mostly men, mostly women, or both men and women in your country? Write *M* (men), *W* (women), or *B* (both men and women).

   _____ Assembly line workers

   _____ Bartenders

   _____ Bus drivers

   _____ Computer programmers

   _____ Lawyers

   _____ Managers

   _____ Physicians

   _____ Secretaries

   _____ Teachers (except college and university)

   _____ Telephone installers and repairers

2. The chart below shows the total percentage of women holding the jobs listed above in the United States. Compare the percentages between 1972 and 1990. In what occupations have women in the United States made the greatest gains since 1972? Why do you think these changes have occurred?

Occupation	1972	1990
Assembly line workers	46.8	43.5
Bartenders	27.9	55.6
Bus drivers	34.1	51.6
Computer programmers	19.9	36.0
Lawyers	4.0	20.6
Managers	INA*	41.0
Physicians	10.1	19.3
Secretaries	99.1	94.5
Teachers (except college and university)	70.0	73.7
Telephone installers and repairers	1.9	11.3

Source: Bureau of Labor and Statistics
*INA = Information not available

3. In what occupations do you think women in your country have made the greatest gains? Why have these changes occurred?

4. Do women hold managerial positions in your country? How common is it for women to hold senior-level decision-making positions in your country?

5. What do you think are the advantages of having women managers and decision makers?

LANGUAGE EXPANSION

Expressions and Idioms

In the United States, it is common to talk about winning or losing negotiations, and terminology used for negotiation is often the same as that used for sports. The expressions in the left-hand column below are used for both sports and negotiation.

Match the expressions to their sports definitions.

_____ 1. a game plan

_____ 2. opponent/opposing team

_____ 3. warm up the opponent

_____ 4. set the ground rules

_____ 5. home court advantage

_____ 6. to strike out

a. in baseball, to swing at and miss the ball three times resulting in an *out*

b. to play better in your own city or country because you know the surroundings (playing field, courts, fans)

c. to review the regulations and rules of the game before the play begins

d. friendly play between the two teams before the game to get to know each other

e. the other person or team

f. strategy you use to try to win a game

Now use the expressions in their negotiation sense by completing the following sentences.

Last year the Christmas Company of Canada tried to negotiate a deal with a Mexican department store. The negotiations took place in Mexico, giving the Mexican team the _____ _____. The Canadian team brought many gifts and samples of their products to give to their _____. This was done as an effort to show cooperation and to _____. After the two teams_____ on how the negotiations would go, they began talking about money. The Mexican team had a definite _____ that included keeping the Canadian team waiting for weeks for a decision. In the end, the Canadian team decided they could not wait anymore and went back to Canada. In this case, both teams _____ because no deal was made.

Word Forms

Often the same base can be used in verb, noun, and adjective form. Complete the following chart with the missing noun and verb forms.

Verb	Noun	Adjective
▓▓▓▓▓▓		competent
know		knowledgeable
	authority	authorized
▓▓▓▓▓▓		ambitious
compete		competitive
create		creative
	training	trainable
persuade		persuasive

Complete the following sentences with the correct verb, noun, or adjective form from the chart above. Use one form of each word base, and do not repeat any words.

1. The manager must _____ any extended vacation an employee requests.

2. The management does a great job_____ their employees for overseas positions.

3. _____ successfully in the international business field, you must have many qualified employees.

4. The businesswoman's speech was very _____ .
   She convinced everyone that her product was the best on the
   market.

5. Yelana is a very successful marketing artist. She can
   _____ new product labels almost overnight.

6. Patricia Delgado is a very _____ supervisor.
   She works thirteen hours a day and never takes lunch. She is
   hoping to be made manager soon.

7. Many businesspeople have no _____
   of overseas business practices. This is why they fail so often.

8. Mr. Cross is not a_____worker. He
   never finishes his jobs and he is always late for work.

■ BIBLIOGRAPHY

Chesanow, Neil. *The World Class Executive,* New York: Rawson
   Associates, 1985.

Copeland, Lennie, and Lewis Griggs. *Going International.* New York:
   Penguin Books, 1985.

Fisher, Glen, *International Negotiations.* Maine: Intercultural Press,
   1980.

Harris, Philip R., and Robert T. Moran. *Managing Cultural Differences.*
   Houston, Texas: Gulf Publishing, 1991.

Hendon, Donald W., and Rebecca Angeles Hendon. *World Class
   Negotiating: Dealmaking in the Global Marketplace.* New York: John
   Wiley & Sons, 1990.

NEGOTIATIONS ACROSS CULTURES

Unit 6

1. Where are these two people? What are they doing?

2. In your country, is it common to negotiate the price of goods in a market?

3. What kinds of products are negotiated in your country?

    ____ food in a restaurant   ____ clothes in a store

    ____ food in a market   ____ a car

    ____ a house   ____ other: _____

4. What kinds of services are negotiable in your country?

    ____ taxi rides   ____ cleaning services

    ____ apartment rent   ____ doctor services

    ____ mechanical repairs   ____ legal services

CASE STUDY

JAPAN AND U.S. CANDY VENTURE

A well-known U.S. candy company was interested in selling its product overseas. The company found a possible **partner** based in Tokyo, Japan. The Tokyo company seemed to be perfect for the deal. After many phone calls between the two parties, a decision was made to meet in Tokyo. The U.S. company chose one of their businessmen, Mike Waller, to represent it in Tokyo. He was the company's most persuasive negotiator.

Before Waller left the United States, he and the company lawyer worked together to write a detailed contract for the deal. The contract was fifty pages long. The deal would be **advantageous** for both companies. It promised big **profits**.

Waller left for Japan with the contract. He was pleased with his careful preparation. He thought his future partners would be satisfied with his work and would be ready **to bargain** about the details in the contract. He had studied their company **interests** and was sure they would want to change a few **conditions** in the contract. He planned to agree to those changes as **concessions**. He was certain the meetings would result in good negotiations and a quick final agreement.

On the day of the meeting in Tokyo, Waller entered the boardroom with copies of the contract for the Japanese businessmen at the meeting. He handed them each a copy and began discussing the details. The representatives of the Tokyo company did not open their contracts. They didn't discuss the contract at all, but instead spoke about general business issues. They spoke about the **proposed** cooperation between the two companies but they didn't make any promises.

Waller then went back to the United States. He felt extremely surprised and disappointed. The Japanese businessmen had never asked him one question about the contract. No agreements or **commitments** had been made. He wasn't even sure if there would be another **round** of negotiations.

Vocabulary

Circle the words that are most similar in meaning to the words in italics (taken from the story).

1. The company found a possible *partner* based in Tokyo, Japan.
   a. friend
   b. part owner of a business venture
   c. buyer

2. The deal would be *advantageous* for both companies.
   a. good
   b. terrible
   c. complicated

3. It promised big *profits* for both parties.
   a. money
   b. future
   c. vacations

4. He thought the Japanese company would be ready *to bargain* about the details in the contract.
   a. make cheaper
   b. discuss the conditions of
   c. think about

5. He had studied their company *interests* and was sure they would want to change a few conditions in the contract.
   a. hobbies
   b. advantages
   c. concerns

6. He was sure they would want to change a few *conditions* in the contract.
   a. provisions
   b. pieces of information
   c. names

7. He planned to agree to those changes as *concessions*.
   a. giving up something to the other side
   b. mistakes
   c. promises

8. The Japanese spoke about the *proposed* cooperation between the two companies, but they didn't make any promises.
    a. impossible
    b. suggested
    c. definite

9. No agreements or *commitments* had been made.
    a. actions
    b. promises
    c. signatures

10. He wasn't even sure if there would be another *round* of negotiations.
    a. circle
    b. series
    c. wheel

Reviewing the Case

Answer the following questions and share your answers with a partner.

1. How did the two companies first communicate with each other?
2. How did the American representative prepare for the first meeting?
3. How did the Japanese businessmen respond to the contract?

Making Inferences

Answer the following questions and share your answers with a partner.

1. Why do you think Mike Waller brought a contract to the first meeting?
2. Why do you think the Japanese representatives didn't look at the contract during the first meeting? What did they expect from that meeting?
3. Why do you think the two parties failed to reach an agreement?

Problem Solving: Information Gap

The two companies are still interested in the proposed deal. They want to understand the differences between the negotiation processes in the two countries, so they may be more successful in their next round of negotiations. As a class you are to investigate the differences and then develop a plan for the next encounter.

Divide the class into two groups: A and B. Group A reads the U.S. cultural information in Appendix Activity 25. Group B reads the Japanese cultural information in Appendix Activity 11. After reading the information, complete your part of the chart below. Next, find a partner from the other group and ask questions to complete the chart.

	In Japan	In the United States
1. Which phases of negotiations are most emphasized? Why?		
2. At what point of the negotiation process are concessions made? What is their role in negotiations?		
3. In what phase do negotiators use a contract? What is its role in negotiations?		
4. How much time does a company spend in negotiations? Why?		

Discussion

Go back to your groups and discuss the following.

1. Now that you have more information about both cultures, do you want to change any of your answers from Making Inferences on page 81? Discuss your changes if any.
2. What difference between the two styles had the most serious effect on the negotiations?
3. What could Mike Waller have done after that first meeting, but before leaving Japan, to improve the relationship?

Written Reflection

The two companies are still interested in this business venture. How can they compromise their negotiating styles in order to work out an agreement with each other more successfully?

Write up a plan for the two companies that will result in a more successful negotiation. Your plan should include a schedule for the number of meetings and an explanation of how each phase of the negotiation process is achieved. To help you prepare your plan, review the issues in the chart above. When you have finished, share your plan with the class.

AROUND THE WORLD

Nonverbal Communication

Almost 70 percent of all communication is nonverbal. Nonverbal communication includes: eye contact, gestures, silence in conversations, and touching. Like verbal communication, nonverbal communication varies culture to culture. One study of Brazilians, Japanese, and Americans in business meetings found great variation in the amount of eye contact, touching, and silence.

NONVERBAL COMMUNICATION IN BUSINESS MEETINGS IN THREE CULTURES

	Japanese	Americans	Brazilians
Silent Periods (Number of silent periods greater than 10 seconds per 30 minutes)	5.5	3.5	0
Conversational Overlaps/Interruptions (Number per 10 minutes)	12.6	10.3	28.6
Facial Gazing (Number of minutes of eye contact per 10 minutes)	1.3	3.3	5.2
Touching (Number per 30 minutes, not including handshaking)	0	0	4.7

Source: John Graham, "The Influence of Culture on the Process of Business Negotiations: An Exploratory Study." *Journal of International Business Studies*, XVI, no.1 (Spring 1985): p. 84.

Discussion

Answer the following questions with a partner.

1. Which culture has the most silence during a business meeting? Which culture has the least silence?
2. In which culture is it most common to speak while someone else is speaking?
3. Which culture has the most facial gazing and touching? Which culture has the least?
4. How could these differences affect a negotiation? What are some problems that might arise in a negotiation between Japanese and Brazilian companies, for example? Do you think these problems could be serious?

Applying Your Knowledge

An American–Japanese Encounter

A U.S. airplane manufacturer and a Japanese airline company were negotiating the price of some airplanes. The American negotiating team suggested a price. In response, the Japanese were quiet. The American team then lowered the price. The Japanese team again were quiet. The American team lowered the price again. The Japanese team continued to keep silent. In the end, the Japanese team came away from the negotiation with a price lower than they ever expected. The Americans were disappointed because they sold the planes at a very low price.

Discuss the following questions. Then go to Appendix Activity 19 for the solution to the case.

1. Why do you think the Americans kept lowering the price?
2. Why do you think the Japanese kept silent?

Your Point of View

EYE CONTACT

Students are in groups of three, with one person as recordkeeper. Two students talk to each other for three minutes. Possible topics to discuss are family, hobbies, travel, school, and studies. The recordkeeper will write down the number of times each student looks in the other student's eyes. As a class discuss the following questions.

1. Which students made the most eye contact?
2. Which students made the least eye contact?
3. At what moments did each student make eye contact (while speaking, while listening, during pauses in the conversation)?
4. What do you think a lot of eye contact in a conversation communicates (interest, aggression, disrespect)?
5. How does your length and frequency of eye contact change when you speak to the following people?
   - your boss
   - your teacher
   - your parents
   - a police officer
   - a stranger
   - someone of the opposite sex

INTERRUPTIONS

Students are in groups of three, with one person as recordkeeper. Two students talk to each other for three minutes. Possible topics to discuss are family, hobbies, travel, school, and studies. The recordkeeper will write down the number of times each student interrupts the other student. As a class discuss the following questions.

1. Which students made the most interruptions?
2. Which students made the least interruptions?
3. How did each person interrupt (by apologizing, by speaking over the other person until the other person stopped speaking, by coughing or somehow indicating the desire to speak)?
4. What do interruptions in a conversation communicate (interest, aggression, disrespect)?

TOUCHING

Do you feel touching is appropriate in the following situations? Discuss your answers in groups.

Touching	Appropriate	Inappropriate
A friend's leg while talking		
A friend's hand while talking		
A friend's arm/shoulder while talking		
A boss's hand while talking		
A boss's arm/shoulder while talking		
A stranger's arm/shoulder while talking		

The Negotiating Table

Nonverbal communication is not limited to gestures, touching, and silence. We also communicate by how we arrange furniture and seat people. Seating arrangements in meetings vary greatly from country to country, company to company, and situation to situation. Generally, some countries, such as Japan, prefer seating arrangements that communicate cooperation. Western countries often prefer seating arrangements that communicate competition.

The following diagrams represent four negotiating table arrangements from around the world. Look at each arrangement and answer the questions in terms of each arrangement. Discuss your answers.

X = Person from country X
O = Person from country O

Arrangement 1

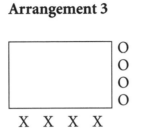

Arrangement 2

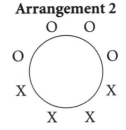

Arrangement 3

Arrangement 4

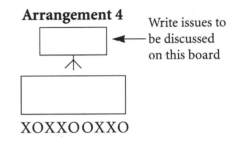

Write issues to be discussed on this board

1. Have you seen this arrangement before? Where?
2. Does the arrangement encourage cooperation or competition? How?
3. What are the advantages and disadvantages of the arrangement?
4. In the space below, draw another possible table arrangement. Is it an arrangement that communicates cooperation or competition? Share your idea with the class.

Your Arrangement

Your Bargaining Style

Now that you have read about many aspects of negotiations, it is time to see what your own style of bargaining is. You will act out a role-play and then reflect on your style of bargaining.

Divide the class in two groups: A and B. Group A reads the seller's information in Appendix Activity 4. Group B reads the buyer's information in Appendix Activity 15. In your group, decide what items are necessary and non-negotiable and what items may be given up in the negotiation as concessions. Next find a partner from the other group and negotiate an agreement. Then write down your agreement in the following table.

Final Agreement of Widget Sale
Price per unit
Conditions of assembly
Terms of payment
Delivery date
Future discounts
Other conditions

Reflection

Think about how you negotiated in the role-play. Complete the following worksheet. Then compare your answers with your partner's.

REFLECTION ON ROLE-PLAY

Styles of Persuasion

How did you try to persuade your partner? Each line below represents a continuum contrasting two different styles of persuasion. Indicate where you fit in, on each line.

cooperative	▬▬▬▬▬▬▬▬▬▬	competitive
spoke indirectly so no one was embarrassed or humiliated	▬▬▬▬▬▬▬▬▬▬	spoke directly
used emotion	▬▬▬▬▬▬▬▬▬▬	used logic
reacted carefully	▬▬▬▬▬▬▬▬▬▬	reacted quickly

Concessions

Did you bargain issue by issue or talk about the whole deal before bargaining?

_____

Did you make many concessions? Did you make them early or late in the negotiation?

_____

Did you reciprocate your partner's concessions?

_____

The Deal

Did you get a good deal? How about your partner?

_____

Was it a successful negotiation? How?

_____

LANGUAGE EXPANSION

Expressions and Idioms

In the United States, negotiations are often seen as similar to a game. Often card game idioms are used to describe what people do when negotiating. Match the idioms with their definitions.

_____ 1. to stack the deck (of cards)

_____ 2. to lay all the cards on the table

_____ 3. to close a deal

_____ 4. to have a poker face

_____ 5. to have a card up one's sleeve

a. to hide something valuable

b. to say something frankly

c. to not show any reaction

d. to trick, to arrange things unfairly

e. to end a negotiation successfully

Complete the following sentences with the correct idioms.

1. We will _____ . We don't have anything to hide from you.

2. I think he _____ . He still hasn't discussed his holdings in that company. I'm sure he has a special deal with someone on the board of directors.

3. She is hard to negotiate with. She _____ . I never know what she is thinking.

4. After they _____ , they all went out to celebrate.

5. The salesman did not tell the customers that the product was damaged. He _____. They found out when they tried to start the machine and it exploded.

Word Forms

Often the same word base can be used in the verb, noun, and adjective form. Complete the following chart with the missing forms.

Verb	Noun	Adjective
arrange		arranged
bargain		
	commitment	committed
	concession	concessionary
process		processed
profit		profitable
propose		proposed

Complete the following sentences with the correct verb, noun, or adjective form of the words in the chart above. Use one form of each word base, and do not repeat any words.

1. The company, in an effort to improve its image in the community, _____ a million dollars to local charities every year.

2. Negotiating in a foreign country is a lengthy _____ _____ . It requires months and even years of research and contact.

3. The company lost money in the fourth quarter. This meant it didn't make any_____this year.

4. The partner _____ that they continue the discussion over dinner.

5. The company was going bankrupt so they sold all their remaining goods at very low prices. They gave some excellent _____ .

(continued on next page)

6. They wanted to close the deal as soon as possible so they
   _____ on many points.

7. The company had _____ for the
   team to stay at the local hotel.

BIBLIOGRAPHY

Adler, Nancy. *International Dimensions of Organizational Behavior.*
Boston: Kent Publishing, 1986.

Barnlund, Dean. *Communicative Styles of Japanese and Americans.*
California: Wadsworth, 1989.

Barnlund, Dean. *Public and Private Self in Japan and United States.*
Tokyo: Simul Press, 1975.

Fisher, Glen. *International Negotiation.* Yarmouth, Maine, USA:
Intercultural Press, 1980.

Frankenstein, John, and Hassan Hosseini, "Advice From the Field:
Essential Training." *Management Review* (July 1988): p. 43.

Fucini, Joseph J., and Suzy Fucini. *Working for the Japanese.* New York:
Free Press, 1990.

Hall, Edward T., and Mildred Reed Hall. *Hidden Differences.* New York:
Anchor Books, 1987.

Moran, Philip R., and William Stripp. *Dynamics of Successful
International Negotiations.* Houston: Gulf Publishing, 1991.

Whitehall, Arthur M. "American Executives Through Foreign Eyes."
Business Horizons (May-June 1989): p. 42-48.

Zimmerman, Mark. *How to do Business with the Japanese.* New York:
Random House, 1985, p. 103.

CONTRACTS ACROSS CULTURES

Unit 7

1. You want to sell your car. You find a buyer and you agree on a price. How do you finalize the agreement? Do you shake hands? Do you sign a paper? Is your agreement verbal (spoken) or written?

2. Look at the following three common ways of finalizing an agreement. Which ones are most common in your country?

   a. handshake

   b. verbal agreement

   c. written contract

3. What type of agreement do you use in the following situations? Write *W* (written), *V* (verbal), or *W* and *V*.

   _____ buying a car

   _____ renting an apartment

   _____ getting a job

   _____ joining a health club

   _____ buying an insurance policy

   _____ obtaining a loan from a bank

   _____ obtaining a loan from a friend or relative

   _____ buying land

WHAT'S IN A HANDSHAKE?

Grand Metropolitan, a British drinks **conglomerate**, wanted to expand. Pernod-Ricard Company of France, another drinks company, also wanted to expand. They were both looking for new companies to invest in. Unfortunately, they both became interested in the same drinks company, which was called Irish Distillers and located in Ireland. But, in order to **take over**, or gain control of, Irish Distillers, they had to first gain control of another company. This company was called FII-Fyffes (pronounced ef-eye-eye-feyefs) and was also in Ireland.

A company takes over another company by buying the majority of **shares**, or **stock**, in that company. FII-Fyffes had the largest number of shares of Irish Distillers stock. The company that bought the most shares of FII-Fyffes would automatically become the largest **shareholders** of Irish Distillers, and in this way would gain control of Irish Distillers.

Grand Metropolitan and Pernod-Ricard were now in competition. Both companies sent representatives to Ireland to try to buy the shares from FII-Fyffes. In one meeting, the representatives of Pernod-Ricard and FII-Fyffes discussed **acceptable** prices for the FII-Fyffes shares. The French company **offered** to pay $4.30 per share. FII-Fyffes **assessed** the offer and then demanded $4.70 per share. Pernod then offered $4.50 per share. The two company representatives shook hands on the $4.50 per share.

The next day, Grand Metropolitan offered FII-Fyffes $5.25 per share. Later that day the Pernod-Ricard and FII-Fyffes representatives met. The FII-Fyffes representative said that the company was rethinking the situation. The Pernod-Ricard representative was shocked.

Pernod-Ricard **brought FII-Fyffes to court**. It demanded that FII-Fyffes honor the handshake the two companies made on the $4.50 per share offer.

Vocabulary

Circle the words or phrases that are most similar in meaning to the words or phrases in italics (taken from the story).

1. Grand Metropolitan, a British drinks *conglomerate*, wanted to expand.
   a. small company providing financial services
   b. large company owned by one person
   c. large company consisting of many smaller companies

2. But, in order to *take over* Irish Distillers, they had to first buy up another company.
    a. to put out of business
    b. gain control of
    c. sell products to

3. A company takes over another company by buying the majority of *shares*, or *stock*, in that company.
    a. parts or portions of a company
    b. products
    c. factories

4. The company that bought many shares of FII-Fyffes would automatically become the largest *shareholders* of Irish Distillers, and in this way would gain control of Irish Distillers.
    a. company
    b. owners of shares
    c. distributors

5. In one meeting, the representatives of Pernod-Ricard and FII-Fyffes discussed *acceptable* prices for the FII-Fyffes shares.
    a. low
    b. agreeable
    c. unsatisfactory

6. The French company *offered* to pay $4.30 per share.
    a. rejected
    b. suggested
    c. agreed

7. FII-Fyffes *assessed* the offer and then demanded $4.70 per share.
    a. rejected
    b. agreed to
    c. considered

8. Pernod-Ricard *brought FII-Fyffes to court.*
    a. held a business meeting with FII-Fyffes
    b. signed a contract with FII-Fyffes
    c. took legal action against FII-Fyffes

Reviewing the Case

Answer the following questions and share your answers with a partner.

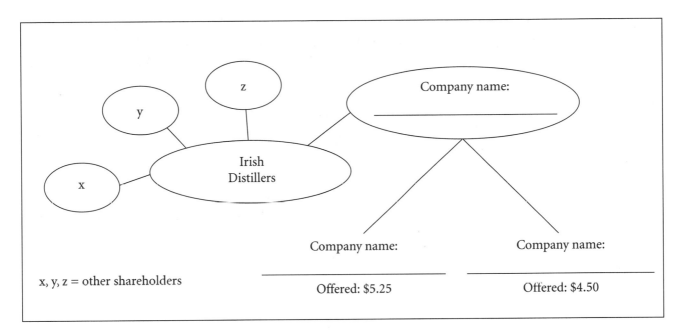

x, y, z = other shareholders

1. Place the three company names on the appropriate lines.
2. Why were Grand Metropolitan and Pernod-Ricard both interested in Irish Distillers?
3. How does one company take over another company?
4. How would Grand Metropolitan and Pernod-Ricard get control over Irish Distillers?
5. Why did Pernod-Ricard bring FII-Fyffes to court?

Making Inferences

Answer the following questions and share your answers with a partner.

1. What do you think a handshake means to Pernod-Ricard?
2. Why do you think FII-Fyffes reconsidered the offer made by Pernod-Ricard?
3. What do you think a handshake means to FII-Fyffes?
4. What do you think FII-Fyffes requires to make a deal binding?

Problem Solving: Role-Play

You and your classmates will act out the meeting between FII-Fyffes and Pernod-Ricard and decide which company should win the case.

Divide the class into three groups, Group A (Pernod-Ricard), Group B (FII-Fyffes), and Group C (mediators). Group A reads their role cards in Appendix Activity 17 and defends their position about the agreement and handshake. Group B reads their role cards in Appendix Activity 27 and defends their position about the agreement and handshake. Group C listens and decides which group should win the case. As the mediators listen to the arguments, they will complete the following chart.

	Pernod-Ricard	FII-Fyffes
1. According to the company, what did its representative think at the end of meeting?		
2. What is the significance of a handshake following an agreement?		
3. How did each representative interpret the handshake? Was it binding?		

Discussion

Go back to your groups, complete the chart, and discuss the following.

1. Which company presented a stronger position? Why was this company's position stronger?
2. Do you think this a case of cross-cultural misunderstanding? Why or why not?
3. Should handshakes and verbal agreements be used in international business negotiations? Why or why not?
4. Why is it important to know about the different forms of agreements (handshakes, written contracts, verbal contracts) in other countries?

Written Reflection

Read the actual solution in Appendix Activity 1. In the case, FII-Fyffes potentially lost millions of dollars. In your opinion, how much responsibility does a company have to know about the other country's culture before doing business with them? Do you think this case and other cases of cross-cultural misunderstanding should go to a legal decision?

Write your answer including an explanation and references to this case as an example. When you have finished, share your written reflection with the class.

AROUND THE WORLD

Explicit and Implicit Styles of Agreements

There are basically two styles of agreements: explicit and implicit. Agreements in an explicit style are written, lengthy, and detailed. Agreements in an implicit style are verbal, brief, and lacking in detail. No agreement is purely explicit or implicit. Every agreement involves parts of both the explicit and implicit styles. The relationship between the two parties making an agreement often helps determine what combination of explicit and implicit styles the agreement has. In addition, different cultures often emphasize one style or the other. Let's look at some differences between the explicit and implicit styles of agreement.

EXPLICIT	IMPLICIT

Relationship of the Parties

• The relationship between the parties is based on the contract	• The relationship is based on personal relations

Communication Between the Parties

• Limited (brief)	• Extensive (lengthy)
• Verbal	• Verbal and nonverbal
• Formal	• Formal and informal

Exchange of Promises in the Contract

• Detailed	• General
• Obligations are carefully explained	• Obligations are not carefully explained
• Breaches are clearly defined	• Breaches are not clearly defined

Time Orientation

• Future can be predicted and is included in the contract	• Future cannot be predicted and is not included in the contract
• Clear beginning and ending to time of agreement	• No clear beginning and ending to time of agreement
• No future relationship or cooperation is assumed after contract is over	• Future relationship and cooperation is assumed after contract is over

Responsibilities of the Two Parties

• Responsibility is only to your company	• Responsibility is to both companies
• Conflicts of interest are accepted	• Conflicts of interest are not common
• Belief that selfishness is natural in business	• Belief in cooperation
• If business transaction doesn't work, each company tries to protect its interests	• If business transaction doesn't work, both companies try to work together to solve the problem

Source: Moran, Robert T. and William G. Stripp. *Dynamics of Successful International Business Negotiations.* Houston: Gulf Publishing Company, 1991. Used with permission. All rights reserved.

Applying Your Knowledge

A U.S.–SAUDI ARABIAN ENCOUNTER

An American clothes manufacturer and a Saudi Arabian clothes distributor came to the end of lengthy negotiations in Saudi Arabia. The American manufacturer was pleased with the negotiations, although they had taken much longer than he had planned. They had finally agreed to prices and methods of distribution. The Saudi Arabian distributor asked the American when he could expect his first shipment of clothes. The American answered that they could begin business only when the contracts were written and signed. The Saudi Arabian businessman said that he thought everything was agreed to and finalized during the negotiations. The American said that was true, but he still insisted on a written contract. The written contract would say exactly when their business would begin and end and state all the terms they had agreed to. When the Saudi Arabian heard this he became extremely insulted. He told the American that he was close to canceling the deal.

Discussion

Answer the following questions as a class. Use the previous chart to help explain your answers.

1. Which style of agreement, explicit or implicit, did the American and the Saudi Arabian have? What are some examples?
2. Why do you think the American businessman would only do business after a written contract was signed?
3. Why do you think the Saudi Arabian was close to canceling the deal?
4. What can the American and the Saudi Arabian do to save their business arrangement? What is a plan that will take into consideration both businessmen's contract styles?

Look at these two contracts with a partner. Answer the following questions together.

1. Which contract looks like a complete contract from beginning to end?

2. Which contract talks about a wide range of possible future situations?

3. Which contract seems to have more details?

4. Which one do you think is more implicit, which one is more explicit? Explain your answer.

EXCERPT FROM AN AMERICAN STYLE CONTRACT

14.1 Should any circumstances preventing the complete or partial fulfillment by either of the parties of the obligations taken under this contract arise, namely: fire, floods, earthquake, typhoon, epidemics and other actions or force of nature, as well as war, military operations of any character, prohibitions of export or import, the time stipulated for the fulfillment of the obligations shall be extended for a period equal to that during which such circumstances will remain in force.

14.2 If these circumstances continue for more than six months, each of the parties shall have the right to refuse in full or in part from any further execution of the obligations under this contract and in such case neither of the parties shall have the right for reimbursement of any possible damages by the other party.

14.3 The party for whom it becomes impossible to meet its obligations under this contract shall immediately advise the other party as regards the commencement and cessation of the circumstances preventing the fulfillment of its obligations.

14.4 The delayed advice of the commencement or cessation of *force majeure* circumstances exceeding 15 days will deprive the party of the right to refer to these circumstances at a later date.

Source: *Smart Bargaining: Doing Business with the Japanese*, Rev. Ed. by John L. Graham and Yoshihiro Sano. Copyright © 1984 by John L. Graham and Yoshihiro Sano. Copyright © 1989 by Ballinger, A Division of Harper & Row, Publishers, Inc. Reprinted by permisssion of HarperCollins Publishers, Inc.

A SAMPLE JAPANESE STYLE CONTRACT

Article 1: This agreement is made this 4th day of October 1989 between "A" located in Tokyo, and "B" located in Shibuya-ku Tokyo, to maintain mutual prosperity and coexistence and lasting amicable relations.

Article 2: B shall continuously develop products based upon all of B's copyrighted materials or designs, and actively conduct sales of such products in Japan and other nations. A shall not, without B's consent, have third parties in the aforementioned areas develop products based upon any of A's copyrighted materials or designs, provided, however, that this limitation shall not apply to written materials.

Article 3: B may register designs to protect B's rights against third parties.

Article 4: The content and proofreading of the said copyrighted materials shall be the responsibility of A.

Article 5: The costs required for the writing of the said copyrighted materials shall be borne by A, and the costs of producing, selling and advertising shall be borne by B.

Article 6: As a royalty for the production of A's coyprighted materials and designs, B shall pay A 3 percent of the cost thereof.

Article 7: With A's consent, B shall have the right to have third parties produce totally or partially products based upon A's copyrighted materials or designs. In such cases, B shall pay A the royalty set forth in Article 6.

Article 8: In the event that either A or B suffers damages due to violation by the other party of the terms set forth in this contract, the first party may claim damages.

Article 9: Two identical counterparts are to be prepared, signed and sealed to evidence this contract, whereupon each party shall retain one copy.

A: _____

B: _____

Honoring Contracts

Regardless of whether a contract is implicit or explicit, exactly what is involved in honoring a contract may depend on the country, as well as on the particular situation and parties involved in the contract. For example, contracts can be inflexible or very flexible; they can be fully binding or less than fully binding. Written and verbal agreements may differ in these respects. Here are some examples showing how contracts are generally honored in various countries.

Read the following information and complete the chart with information from your country and your classmate's country.

Middle East	The spoken word is often honored and followed more than the written word. It is common to continue negotiating what is in the contract even after a contract has been written and signed.
Nigeria	Contracts are written or verbal, but the spoken word is often more important than the written word. Both types of contracts are very flexible and change as the situation changes.
Mexico	The written word is more binding than the verbal word. The verbal word is used to ease relationships and not as a verbal contract. The written contract is flexible and changes as the situation changes.
United States	The written word is the most binding. The verbal word is not trusted. Written contracts are not flexible or easy to change.
Your country	
Your classmate's country	

Your Point of View

Read the situations described below and decide what you would do in each situation. Share your answers in groups.

Situation 1

You have decided to sell your car. You put an advertisement in the paper, and yesterday someone came to look at the car. That person offered you a fair price for the car and you agreed to the price. You both decided that he would come back in a few days to pick up the car and pay for it. Today, someone else came by after seeing your car in the driveway. He, too, was interested, and he offered you a higher price than the person yesterday. What will you do? Why?

Situation 2

You have been looking for a job for over a year. Last week you had a job interview, and yesterday the company called you to offer you the position. You went to the office, agreed to a salary, and signed a contract. Today another company called you and offered you a position with them. The position interests you more than the one you agreed to take. It offers more money and prestige. What will you do? Why?

Discussion

Answer the following questions as a class.

1. Do you think verbal and written contracts should differ in how binding they are? Why or why not?

    Do you think verbal and written contracts should differ in how flexible they are? Why or why not?

2. What do you think are the advantages of a contract being flexible?

    What do you think are the advantages of a contract being binding?

3. Have you ever broken a verbal contract? If so, what happened?

    Have you ever broken a written contract? If so, what happened?

LANGUAGE EXPANSION

Expressions and Idioms

In the United States, idioms with the word *word* are used frequently. Here are some examples of these idioms.

Match the idioms to their definitions.

_____ 1. live up to your word/ be as good as your word

_____ 2. actions speak louder than words

_____ 3. take someone at his or her word

_____ 4. give your word of honor

_____ 5. go back on your word

_____ 6. have the last word

a. to make a promise

b. to believe what someone says

c. what you say (you are going to do) is less important than what you do

d. to keep a promise

e. to be the person who makes the final decision

f. to break a promise

Replace the word or phrase in italics with the correct idiom.

1. A: Are you sure the computer will arrive tomorrow?

   B: Absolutely. I *promise.*

   A: Well, that's what you told me last week. I'll believe you when I see the computer here tomorrow.

2. A: Is Mr. Morris really going to give us a discount?

   B: Of course he will. He has always *done what he has promised.*

3. A: Can I have your word that the prices will not go up?

   B: You can be sure. I would never *break a verbal contract.*

4. A: Do you really *trust what he says?*

   B: I don't know yet. I have never done business with him before. But, don't worry. We will *make the decisions*, not him."

Word Forms

Often the same base can be used in verb, noun, and adjective form. Complete the following chart with the missing noun and verb forms.

Verb	Noun	Adjective
	assessment	assessable
	detail	detailed
emphasize		emphatic
oblige		obligatory
	prediction	predictable
transact		transactional
	final	final
	bind	binding

Complete the following sentences with the correct verb, noun, or adjective form from the chart above. Use one form of each word base, and do not repeat any words.

1. Because the future is not entirely _____ , many cultures do not include specifics about the future in their contracts.

2. The _____ of the contract is on quality, not timing. Obviously, quality is the company's main concern.

3. The $4.50 price that Pernod-Ricard offered was their _____ offer. They did not want to offer a higher price.

4. The manager's memos were very _____ . That is why they were always so long.

5. When the company _____ any offer, they think about all the positive and negative points including the effect on future relationship.

6. After the contract ended, the companies had no further _____ to each other.

7. Because the workers wanted to have vacations at different times of the year, they fought for a contract that would not _____ them into taking all of their vacation in August only.

8. Improved relations between the two countries led to a greater number of business _____ between their companies.

BIBLIOGRAPHY

Copeland, Lennie, and Lewis Griggs. *Going International.* New York: Penguin Books, 1985.

Graham, John L., and Yoshiro Sano. *Smart Bargaining: Doing Business with the Japanese.* New York: Harper and Row, 1989.

Harris, Philip R., and Robert T. Moran. *Managing Cultural Differences.* Houston: Gulf Publishing, 1991.

Kennedy, Gavin. *Doing Business Abroad.* New York: Simon and Schuster, 1985.

Moran, Philip R., and William Stripp. *Dynamics of Successful Business Negotiations.* Houston: Gulf Publishing, 1991.

Victor, David A. *International Business Communications.* New York: Harper Collins, 1992.

MARKETING
ACROSS
CULTURES

Unit 8

1. In what country is McDonald's based?
2. Where do you think this McDonald's restaurant is?
3. Are there any McDonald's restaurants in your country?
4. Have you eaten at McDonald's in different countries?
   a. Does the food taste different at McDonald's in different countries? How?
   b. Does the menu offer a different selection of food in different countries?
   c. What remains the same about McDonald's restaurants across cultures?
5. Why do you think McDonald's has been so successful worldwide?

CASE STUDY

BLUE DIAMOND ALMONDS

What is the difference between the U.S. and Canadian markets? Not much, most people would say. But Blue Diamond, a food company based in California, found that there are indeed significant differences. Blue Diamond had run a successful advertising **campaign** for its almonds in the United States. The TV ads used American almond farmers and a humorous **message**. But when tested in Canada, the same **commercials** didn't work. The Canadians found the ads too silly. They also said they prefer to buy products from Canadian farmers. So Blue Diamond hired a local advertising agency to create commercials that **targeted** its Canadian market. The new commercials expressed positive feelings for Canadians in both French and English. They used Shakespeare, Napoleon, and Michelangelo's *David* to **promote** "Blue Diamond Almonds—The Classic Snack." Since the development of this promotional campaign, Blue Diamond's sales in Canada have increased.

This is just one example of Blue Diamond's ability to adapt to different market tastes and **trends**. As a matter of fact, Blue Diamond has become so successful that it now exports 70 percent of its almonds to more than 90 different countries. It says the key to opening markets is market **research.** In each market it hires local agencies to research the region. The local agencies then develop a marketing **strategy** to plan how they will introduce the product and sell it. This process of research, planning, and testing can take as long as five years.

The product, as well as its ads, must be adapted to reach new markets. In the United States, Blue Diamond offers eight different almond flavors that **appeal to** American tastes. The flavors include a spicy barbeque and a ranch style. In Japan it markets twelve different products, eight of which were developed just for the Japanese market. An example is *Calmond*, a snack of cut almonds and dried sardines. Another example is a miso soup mix with almonds. Blue Diamond also produces an almond cracker for Japan's many cracker **consumers**. In Mexico, Blue Diamond markets lemon and chili flavored almonds. In Korea, it markets soy flavored almonds. In Saudi Arabia it markets sweet honey almonds and in Canada it markets a salt and vinegar flavor.

Blue Diamond packaging also varies around the world. The words on the Blue Diamond can are translated into eighteen different languages. The actual can is smaller and thinner in Korea and Japan because consumers have less space for storage. Blue Diamond also plans to market the smaller can in Eastern Europe, so the product will be more affordable.

Vocabulary

Match the following words (taken from the story) to their definitions.

_____ 1. campaign

_____ 2. message

_____ 3. commercials

_____ 4. target

_____ 5. promote

_____ 6. trends

_____ 7. research

_____ 8. strategy

_____ 9. appeal to

_____ 10. consumers

a. attract, to please

b. people who buy products or services

c. current fashions

d. advertisements on TV or radio

e. encourage product sales

f. a plan

g. studying and testing

h. aim at a group of consumers

i. the communication of an idea or information

j. a program for promoting a product or person

Reviewing the Case

Give one example of how Blue Diamond adapted its strategy to its different markets for each of the following aspects of marketing.

Promotion:

Product:

Package:

Making Inferences

"FAMILY I"
QCCO 3007

GROWER: Hi, we're almond growers. We always have almonds around the house.

WIFE: Usually, not this many.

GROWER: Kathy says I bring my work home with me.

Now, I love almonds. I love 'em plain, salted, smokehouse... whatever. I love 'em all.

WIFE: But we can't eat 'em all.

GROWER: That's where you come in. Help us out here, will ya?

ANNCR: (VO) Blue Diamond Almonds. Eight great tastes. And lower prices, too.

GROWER: A can a week, that's all we ask.

Printed with permission from Blue Diamond Growers.

Look at the advertisement for Blue Diamond in the United States. Answer the following questions with a partner.

1. Do you like this ad? Why or why not?
2. Why do you think Americans liked this ad so much?
3. This ad targeted people with a high-middle income. Do you think this ad would be successful in that market in your country? Why or why not?

Problem Solving: Presentations

Good Earth Peanuts wants to start exporting overseas. It would like to duplicate Blue Diamond's success in the world market. The company has hired you to develop a marketing strategy for promoting its product as a snack food in your country.

With two or three other students from your country, develop a promotional campaign for Good Earth Peanuts. Begin by discussing the questions in Appendix Activity 26 with your country in mind. Write out a campaign strategy covering all the questions. Then produce an advertisement to use in the campaign. Present your promotional campaign and your advertisement to the class. The class will listen to each presentation and ad, and will complete the chart below.

Presentation 1	Presentation 2	Presentation 3
Market	Market	Market
Image	Image	Image
Flavors of Product	Flavors of Product	Flavors of Product
Package	Package	Package
Medium of Ad	Medium of Ad	Medium of Ad
Message in Ad	Message in Ad	Message in Ad

Discussion

Look at the completed chart and discuss each of the presentations as a class. Then discuss the following questions.

1. If the students in your class are from different cultures, did you see any differences in their marketing campaigns? What were the differences? Were they significant?
2. Which campaign do you think would be most effective for its market? Why?
3. Could any of the campaigns presented in class be used worldwide? What made their appeal universal?

AROUND THE WORLD

Global Marketing

There are some products that can be marketed around the globe without much variation in the marketing strategy or ad campaign. These are usually durable goods that vary little between markets (e.g., machine parts) or flagship brands that are known across borders. One example of such a brand is Coca-Cola. Coke uses the same strategy from country to country and it often uses the same commercials, just translating them into different languages. Other products that have standardized marketing campaigns include Unilever detergents, Marlboro cigarettes, Perrier water, Kellogg's Frosted Flakes, Pond's skin creams, Ajax cleaners, Canada Dry mixers, Exxon oil, Levi's blue jeans, and British Airways. This trend toward standardized marketing is growing.

Reasons

There are several reasons why companies are turning to global marketing. First of all, it is less expensive. It saves time and money if a company only needs to translate its advertisements in different markets. Second, a unified market is growing across country borders. This market is created in part by global media, such as Rupert Murdoch's Sky Channel, Ted Turner's TBS channel, CNN, and Music Box and MTV, which are both music video channels. These international channels show the same programs everywhere. A new generation of consumers follows the same trends whether they live in Sweden or Colombia. Third, as consumers increase their international travel, companies want them to recognize their products across country lines. As the world gets smaller, companies try to maintain brand consistency.

Obstacles

There are, however, obstacles to the global strategy. Some of the obstacles relate to the products themselves. Certain products, such as unprocessed foods, are difficult to market through a standardized approach. People don't change eating habits readily. Companies usually need to use local strategies for this kind of product. Other obstacles relate to the ad campaigns. Some countries limit or altogether prohibit commercials on TV. A company that depends on a standardized TV ad may have to adapt its ad to other media in these countries. Also many countries require local participation in advertisements so that often ads must be remade locally. Countries also vary on what they consider acceptable advertising material. In the United States and Asia, partial nudity in general advertising is not acceptable; in western Europe it is. Finally, some countries prohibit advertisements that do not reflect local culture, as they fear colonization of the local culture.

Discussion

Discuss the following questions as a class.

1. In what way do you think channels like MTV and CNN contribute to a global market?
2. Do you know of any other recent technical developments that contribute to rapid world communication? How will these new developments affect the new global market?
3. What age group often is the target of global marketing? As this market grows older do you think it will continue to have uniform tastes? Why don't the companies try to market to the older generations?
4. Has your government tried to restrict international advertising campaigns? What do you think of such restrictions?
5. Do you think global marketing can affect local culture? If so how?
6. Do you think local culture can be expressed in advertising? If so, how?

Global and National Brands

QUEBEC, CANADA

Using local strategies to sell a product is not that easy, as the following case demonstrates.

Dow Breweries, a large multinational corporation, introduced a new beer in Quebec, Canada, called Kebec. To appeal to the local pride in Quebec's unique cultural heritage, the beer promotions used the national flag and nationalistic images. Major local groups protested the "profane" use of "sacred" national symbols. The company stopped the campaign after only fifteen days.[1]

Your Point of View

Global brands use the same brand name around the world. National brands are brand names only known in one country. They are produced by smaller companies that only dominate the local market.

Form small groups of students from your country. Decide what the five top global brands are in the world. Then decide what the five top national brands are in your country.

GLOBAL BRANDS	NATIONAL BRANDS
_____	_____
_____	_____
_____	_____
_____	_____
_____	_____

[1]David Ricks, *Big Business Blunders*, Dow Jones-Irwin, 1983.

Discussion

Look at the list of top ten global brands in Appendix Activity 30. Then discuss the following questions.

1. In your list, did you identify all the top global brands? Were there any surprises?
2. Are the global brand products different from the national brand products? If so, how?
3. Do you think the target audience is different for the national and global brands? If so, how?
4. What kind of image do the global brands market in your country? Do the global brands market themselves as universal? Is that to their advantage?
5. What kind of image do the national brands market in your country? Do they market themselves as being local? Is that to their advantage?
6. In what cases is a global image helpful to sales? In what cases is a local image helpful to sales?

LANGUAGE EXPANSION

Expressions and Idioms

The word *market* has many different definitions and is used in various idioms. Match the following idioms to their definitions.

_____ 1. flea market

_____ 2. in the market for

_____ 3. to play the market

_____ 4. buyer's market

_____ 5. on the market

a. a market that favors the consumer not the seller

b. an open air market where antiques and second-hand things are sold

c. ready to buy

d. for sale

e. to try to make money on the stock market by buying and selling stocks

Complete the sentences with the above expressions.

1. The recession has brought house prices down and now that the interest rates are low it is a _____. This is the time to get a house.

2. We just put the new line of products _____ _____. Now they just have to watch to see if consumers will buy them.

3. When we traveled there we visited all the _____ _____ and got the best bargains in town.

4. When interest rates are low, many people start to _____ in hopes of making some money on their savings. It's risky business.

5. People are always _____ good entertainment.

Word Forms

Often the same base can be used in the verb, noun, and adjective form. Complete the following chart with the missing forms.

Verb	Noun	Adjective
prohibit		prohibited
	promotion	promotional
	consumer	consumable
restrict		restrictive
	standard	standard
target		targeted

Complete the following sentences with the correct verb, noun, or adjective form of the words from the chart on page 122. Use one form of each word base, and do not repeat any words.

1. If a company can _____ its products, instead of producing different versions of these products, then it will be able to reduce its expenses.

2. In Muslim states, such as Saudi Arabia, the importation of alcohol is _____ . Absolutely no alcohol is allowed.

3. Market tests showed that _____ didn't like the flavor of the new product.

4. Commercials often _____ teenagers, who are seen as having money to spend and not being already loyal to specific brands.

5. They _____ their products with advertising on radio and in newspapers but sales didn't increase.

6. All countries have _____ on what is permitted in an ad, but these vary from country to country.

BIBLIOGRAPHY

Allen, Gray. "Every Market Needs A Different Message." *ABC Communication World* (April 1990) 16–18.

Alsop, Ronald, and Bill Abrams. *The Wall Street Journal on Marketing.* Homewood, Illinois: Dow Jones–Irwin, 1986.

James, William L., and John S. Hill. "International Advertising Messages: To Adapt or Not to Adapt." *Journal of Advertising Research* (June/July 1991) 65–71.

Lev, Michael. "Advertisers Seek Global Messages." *The New York Times*, National Ed. (11 November, 1991) C7.

Magnier, Mark. "California Almond Cooperative Goes Nuts about Overseas Sales." *Journal of Commerce and Commercial* (10 October 1990) 5A.

Mazur, Laura, and Annik Hogg. *The Marketing Challenge.* England: Addison-Wesley, 1993.

MANAGEMENT AND EMPLOYEE RELATIONS ACROSS CULTURES

Unit 9

1. Who is the manager in the picture? How can you tell?
2. The following is a short description of three different management styles. Check the one you think is being used in the meeting.

   _____ **Autocratic:** The manager tells the workers exactly what to do. Workers have little or no participation at any level of decision making.

   _____ **Democratic or Participative:** The manager asks workers for opinions and ideas to solve problems. The manager often makes the final decisions, although at times, the workers may have decision-making power.

   _____ **Laissez Faire:** The manager gives all decision-making power to the workers. The manager has little control or input.

3. What management style are you most familiar with?

CASE STUDY

ARE TWO MANAGERS TOO MANY?

Three years ago, a German manufacturer of domestic electrical appliances (hairdryers, blenders, coffee grinders, etc.) opened a **plant** in Tijuana, Mexico.

The company has two **assembly line** managers; one is German and one is Mexican. Nine months ago, a new German assembly line manager was sent over to replace a returning manager. The returning manager was not successful with managing the assembly line employees during his stay. The new manager is Ms. Mara Graus. Working alongside Ms. Graus is the Mexican manager, Pablo Arango, who has been at the plant from the beginning. Both managers share responsibilities. They are responsible for teaching the German-based assembly line technology to the workers. They are also responsible for four floor **supervisors** who **oversee** the thirty assembly line workers.

From the beginning the two managers have disagreed on many management **policy** issues:

Ms. Graus feels that Mr. Arango is too friendly with **subordinates**, both the supervisors and assembly line workers. Mr. Arango, in contrast, feels that Ms. Graus is very cold and unfriendly to subordinates.

Mr. Arango feels that the floor supervisors should be given more responsibility and control over their workers. He feels they should be given more information related to their jobs and more decision-making power. Ms. Graus feels that they have enough information to carry out their jobs and that she and Mr. Arango should be making all the decisions.

Ms. Graus feels that the assembly line workers have low company **morale**. She believes that competitions in which workers with the greatest **output** are rewarded with a **bonus** would raise company spirits. Mr. Arango feels such competitions actually lower morale not raise it.

The disagreements have become so serious that Ms. Graus and Mr. Arango are no longer able to effectively manage the assembly line.

Vocabulary

Match the following words (taken from the story) to their definitions.

_____ 1. plant

_____ 2. assembly line

_____ 3. supervisor

_____ 4. oversee

_____ 5. policy

_____ 6. subordinate

_____ 7. morale

_____ 8. output

_____ 9. bonus

a. area of a factory responsible for putting together or constructing goods

b. amount produced

c. person who works for another

d. methods, procedures

e. director, person in charge of workers

f. factory

g. state of mind and spirit of a group

h. a reward, sometimes monetary

i. direct

Reviewing the Case

Answer the following questions and share your answers with a partner.

1. What are Ms. Graus and Mr. Arango's responsibilities as managers?
2. What are some of the problems the two managers have with each other? Complete the chart below.

	Ms. Graus Says	**Mr. Arango Says**
Subordinates	_Mr. Arango is too friendly._	
Control		
Competition		

Making Inferences

Answer the following questions. Share your answers.

1. Which management style described on page 126 do you think Ms. Graus has? Mr. Arango?
2. What reasons do you think Ms. Graus might have for not being friendly with subordinates? What reasons do you think Mr. Arango might have for being friendly with subordinates?
3. What reasons do you think Ms. Graus might have for wanting to keep control and decision-making power? What reasons do you think Mr. Arango might have for not wanting to give supervisors more control and decision-making power?
4. Why might a competition raise or lower morale?

Problem Solving: Information Gap

Mr. Arango and Ms. Graus have both written letters to the bosses at their respective headquarters. The bosses have asked you and your classmates to read the letters and help them solve the problems between Mr. Arango and Ms. Graus.

Divide the class into two groups: A and B. Group A reads the letter from Ms. Graus in Appendix Activity 14 and Group B reads the letter from Mr. Arango in Appendix Activity 7. After reading the information, complete your part of the chart below. Next, find a partner from the other group and ask questions to complete the chart.

	Ms. Graus	Mr. Arango
1. How does a manager gain respect and trust from an employee?		
2. What is the ideal relationship between manager and employee? Is it personal, distant, social, formal?		
3. Who should make the decisions and hold the information? Why?		
4. Is competition at work among employees useful? Why or why not?		

Discussion

Go back to your groups, look at the completed chart, and discuss the following.

1. Now that you have more information about both cultures, do you want to change any of your answers from Making Inferences on page 129? Discuss your changes if any.
2. What difference between the two managers do you think has the most serious effect on their working together?
3. What are the advantages and disadvantages of the two different styles of management?

Written Reflection

In the case, two managers worked together, one from the host country (Mexico) and the other from the home country (Germany). This type of dual management is popular in many international companies. It has many advantages, but it can be difficult to blend the personal management styles of both people. In addition, if the two countries the managers are from tend to favor different management styles, the likelihood of disagreements between the two managers increases. To what extent should the management style reflect the style of the home country? How much should the management style reflect the style of the host country?

Write a management plan for the Tijuana plant that will resolve the differences between Ms. Graus and Mr. Arango so that they can manage the plant more successfully. To help you organize your plan, review the issues in the above chart. When you have finished, share your plan with the class.

AROUND THE WORLD

Decision-Making and Management Styles

Management style depends on both individual and cultural factors. Each manager has a different way of managing the people who work for him or her, but at the same time, many cultures have a dominant management style. For example, in Saudi Arabia and Nigeria, many managers make all the decisions without the workers' input. They feel they are responsible for making decisions that are best for the workers, much like a parent's relationship to his or her own children. In Japan, many managers ask their workers for their input before making a decision. Group consensus about a decision is more important than what one individual thinks is right.

The following chart shows a range of management styles and how these styles affect the way decisions are made.

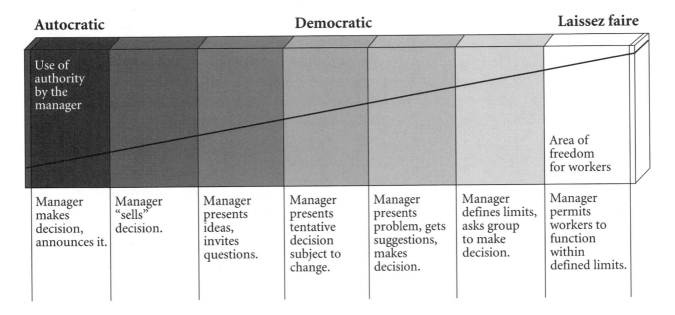

David Rachman, *Business Today*, 1990, McGraw-Hill, Inc. Reproduced with permission.

Discussion

Answer the following questions in groups.

1. Read the following opinions of three different workers about decision making. Which management style does he or she like? Which opinion do you agree with most and why? Which opinion do you disagree with most and why?

   a. The more people involved with making a decision the better. We can get as many ideas as possible and be sure we are thinking of everything. After we have shared our ideas, the management should make the final decision based on what is best for the company.

   b. Everyone should share equal decision-making power. We are more apt to accept decisions if they are made by us. In this way we stay in control of our environment, making us happier workers.

   c. Decisions are best made by one person who really knows his or her workers and all of the issues involved. In this way, decisions are made faster and our work can continue uninterrupted.

2. If you are (were) working under another person, what kind of management style does (did) your boss have? Where would he or she fit on the continuum?

3. Do you think your culture has a dominant management style? If yes, describe it. If no, what are some of the different styles you can see in your culture?

4. Do you think that managers should follow a consistent style or that different styles are appropriate in different circumstances? Explain your answer.

Applying Your Knowledge

This role-play will show you how different management styles affect worker involvement and satisfaction. Follow the directions carefully.

In groups of at least three people, you will work on three different projects using paper and tape. Choose three people to be managers: A, B, and C. Each manager will manage a different paper project. Manager A reads the information in Appendix Activity 16. Manager B reads the information in Appendix Activity 13. Manager C reads the information in Appendix Activity 20. Manager A will direct his or her project first followed by manager B and then manager C. During each project the group (workers) will listen to the manager's instructions. After you complete the three projects, fill in the questionnaire on page 133 and share your answers with the class.

Manager A will supervise Project 1, making paper sailing ships.

Manager B will supervise Project 2, making paper boxes.

Manager C will supervise Project 3, making paper hats.

Questionnaire for Management Role-Play

Discuss the questions in your group and circle the best response on the right.

	Project 1	Project 2	Project 3
1. Did your manager ask for your opinions and suggestions?	Frequently Sometimes Never	Frequently Sometimes Never	Frequently Sometimes Never
2. Did your manager listen to your opinions and suggestions?	Frequently Sometimes Never	Frequently Sometimes Never	Frequently Sometimes Never
3. Did you use the workers' opinions and suggestions?	Frequently Sometimes Never	Frequently Sometimes Never	Frequently Sometimes Never
4. Who was in control of your project?	Manager Manager and Workers Workers	Manager Manager and Workers Workers	Manager Manager and Workers Workers
5. What kind of manager do you think you had?	A D L*	A D L	A D L

*A = Autocratic, D = Democratic, L = Laissez faire

Your Point of View

After completing all three role plays, you should have a good idea of what the three different management styles are like.

Answer the following questions in *new* groups.

1. Which project was the fastest? Which management style was used? Why was it so fast?
2. Which project was the slowest? Which management style was used? Why was it so slow?
3. What are the positive and negative points of each management style?
4. Which management style would you like to work under? Why?

Management and Employee Relations — Employee Programs

In the case study, Mr. Arango and Ms. Graus were both concerned with employee satisfaction and morale. A big issue these days in U.S. businesses is how to keep employees satisfied. It is believed that employees who are satisfied will be more productive and loyal to the company. This means employees will take fewer sick days, come to work on time, and be able to deal with their work better. Some companies therefore offer a range of programs to promote employee satisfaction and well-being. The chart gives some examples of these programs.

Read the chart and indicate whether the programs are common, occasional, or rare in your country. Share your answers with the class.

Program Offered:	In My Country, This Program Is:
1. **Day care or child care:** Employees' preschool children are taken care of at the workplace in a special center.	____ common ____ occasional ____ rare
2. **Child care grants:** Money is given by the company to the employee to help pay for child care away from the workplace during parent's work hours.	____ common ____ occasional ____ rare
3. **Family leave:** Employees are given time off for maternity leave, being new fathers, or taking care of sick relatives.	____ common ____ occasional ____ rare
4. **Fitness centers:** Gyms and fitness classes are provided at the workplace or employees are given memberships or membership discounts to fitness centers away from the workplace.	____ common ____ occasional ____ rare
5. **Counseling:** The company provides counseling about different social issues, for example, eldercare (caring for elderly parents), alcoholism, and child care.	____ common ____ occasional ____ rare
6. **Flexible work hours:** Employees start and finish work earlier or later in the day depending on their needs (for example, 7:00-3:00, 8:00-4:00, 10:00-6:00).	____ common ____ occasional ____ rare
7. **Job-sharing:** Two people share one job working on different days or at different times of the day.	____ common ____ occasional ____ rare

Your Point of View

Work in groups of three or four people. Imagine that your group is a management team in charge of selecting special programs to offer employees. Decide which programs from the chart you would like to offer. Rank your choices from most important to least important. Be sure to consider the following points:

- How does the employee benefit from the program?
- How does the company benefit from the program?

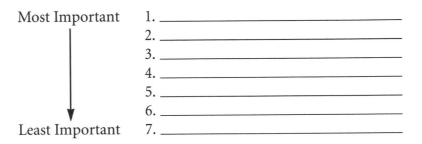

Share your answers and explain your choices to the class. As a class, choose four of the most important programs and rank them below starting with the most important one.

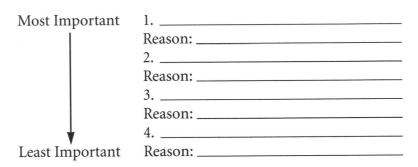

Discussion

Answer the following questions as a class.

1. If you are working or have worked, what kind of employee programs do you or have you had?

2. Are there any employee programs that companies in your country must offer because of government laws (e.g., maternity leave, day care) ?

3. What type of employee programs would you like to have in your ideal job?

LANGUAGE EXPANSION

Expressions and Idioms

In the United States, decision making at work is often done in group meetings. Participants at these meetings often have certain roles they play. Some participants like to speak a lot and give their opinions, others like to listen, and yet others like to criticize and point out the problems with other people's opinions. Of course people do not play the same role in every meeting, but roles can change from moment to moment or even from meeting to meeting. The following terms are used to describe some of the roles.

Match the following expressions to their definitions.

_____ 1. gatekeeper

_____ 2. driver

_____ 3. blocker

_____ 4. harmonizer

_____ 5. tap dancer

_____ 6. fence sitter

a. a person who won't commit to either side of an issue

b. a person who tries to find the good in everyone's opinion and to keep conflict away from the group

c. a person who makes sure that everyone in the group has a chance to participate and no one person has the control

d. a person who avoids giving opinions and answers

e. a person who pushes the group forward to complete the task

f. a person who stops the meeting from continuing until his or her opinion is addressed

The following is the secretary's notes of a meeting held by a group of managers. The managers were discussing possible pay raises for the next year.

Read the report and complete the sentences that follow by deciding which role each manager played in the meeting.

DATE: January 4, 1995
SUB: Pay raises for following year
IN ATTENDANCE: Chris, Paula, Harold, Andrew, Shari, Steven

The meeting started with Chris asking everyone what their ideas were for the pay raises. Everyone responded with ideas except for Paula, who said she would rather listen to everyone else's opinions first and who never did give any opinion. Harold refused to go on with the meeting until his idea of combining holiday leave with pay raises was discussed fully. When the group started talking about how many holidays the next year had, Andrew reminded them that they were there to talk about the raises, not holidays. Shari stated that Harold, like everyone else, had a good point and that it should be addressed at another meeting. At the end of the meeting Steven said that he could not make any decisions today. He would think about all that was discussed and get back to the group next week with an answer.

In the meeting:

1. Chris was a _____.

2. Paula was a _____.

3. Harold was a _____.

4. Andrew was a _____.

5. Shari was a _____.

6. Steven was a _____.

Word Forms

Often the same base can be used in verb, noun, and adjective form. Complete the following chart with the missing forms.

Verb	Noun	Adjective
adjust		adjustable
supervise	supervisor	
	satisfaction	satisfactory
subordinate		
	domination	dominating/ dominant
motivate		motivational
	consultant	consulting

Complete each sentence with the correct verb, noun, or adjective form of the words in the chart above. Use one form of each word base, and do not repeat any words.

1. Pedro is a very _____ manager. He never lets anyone else give their opinions or suggestions in the weekly meetings.

2. The _____ of the assembly line had a meeting to discuss their poor output.

3. The workers had nothing _____ them to do a good job. The pay was low, and the benefits were terrible.

4. Sandra had a hard time _____ to the demands of her new management job. She was very uncomfortable telling her subordinates what to do.

5. Ms. Estey is popular with her _____ , who feel she makes them work hard but is also very fair.

6. The employees were not _____
   before the pay raises were decided. They would never have
   agreed to such a low pay raise.

7. Juan Carlos did not get a very good year-end review. His
   manager said his work was not _____ .

BIBLIOGRAPHY

Chesanow, Neil. *The World Class Executive.* New York: Rawson
   Associates, 1985.

Kras, Eva. *Management In Two Cultures.* Yarmouth, Maine, USA:
   Intercultural Press, 1988.

Mole, John. *When in Rome.* New York: American Management
   Association, 1991.

Moran, Robert T., and Philip R. Harris. *Managing Cultural Synergy.*
   Houston: Gulf Publishing, 1982.

THE INTERNATIONAL BUSINESSPERSON ACROSS CULTURES

Unit 10

1. To be successful in the international business world, businesspeople need to have the skills or abilities listed below. You also use these skills when you are with people from other nationalities in the workplace and even outside the workplace. Think of some examples of where you have used the following skills from your office, in your classroom, during international travel, and at a restaurant. Share your examples with your classmates.

   - **Communication skills:** skills in listening, speaking, and writing to others in order to exchange information effectively
   - **Interpersonal skills:** skills in dealing with people, cooperating with them, and being sensitive to people's needs
   - **Cross-cultural skills:** skills in relating to people of different nationalities and cultures, especially by understanding their beliefs and values

2. What other skills do you think international businesspeople need?

3. Where and how do people acquire the skills mentioned?

4. What can people do to improve their skills?

CASE STUDY

WHOM SHOULD WE HIRE?

AgroWorld Inc. is a multinational company that produces **agricultural** products. Its main products are **pesticides.** AgroWorld has its headquarters in London and has plants in various parts of the world.

AgroWorld was founded in 1950. For a long time, it was one of the fastest growing, most reputable companies in the industry. Then, in 1973, disaster struck at its Mexico City plant. Highly **toxic** chemical waste from the plant **leaked** into the surrounding farmlands. The leakage destroyed the farmlands and killed many farm animals. The Mexican government forced AgroWorld to shut down the plant. AgroWorld left Mexico in shame after paying millions of dollars to the community to **compensate** for the damages. The story was covered worldwide, and raised anger and concern across Latin America.

Since 1973, AgroWorld has not had any problems. As part of its expansion and globalization plan for the 1990s, it is opening a plant outside of Quito, Ecuador. The plant will employ over 700 people and **incorporate** the newest technology in the industry. This technology is designed to prevent any leakage such as that in Mexico. The company is very aware of the community's sensitivity to the Mexico disaster and is trying to do everything possible to become a welcome member of the community.

The company is now in the process of hiring a public relations (PR) person. This person will act as a **liaison**, or bridge, between the company and the world and, especially, between the company and the local community. The position is a **challenging** one because the community is divided over the building of the plant. Some people want the plant because it will provide job opportunities and attract other industry to the area. Others argue that the plant could cause serious **damage** to the community's health and farmlands as it did in Mexico. These people are especially concerned about the new technology because it has never been used before. In order to convince them that they are wrong, the PR person must promote and explain the company's new technology. Promotion is done through **press releases** in the international, national, and local newspapers as well as through visits and lectures to local schools and businesses.

The PR person has many other responsibilities as well. He or she must report back to top management at headquarters in London. Moreover, AgroWorld would like to build goodwill locally by donating money to be used for a health clinic, sports center, or community center. These projects can be successful in building goodwill only if the PR person has been able to develop strong relationships with and win the trust of the community.

Vocabulary

Match the following words (taken from the story) to their definitions.

_____ 1. agricultural

_____ 2. pesticides

_____ 3. toxic

_____ 4. leak

_____ 5. compensate

_____ 6. incorporate

_____ 7. liaison

_____ 8. challenge

_____ 9. damage

_____ 10. press release

a. injure, or to harm

b. contact, connection

c. include

d. escape accidentally, to let out

e. difficult or demanding

f. farming

g. poisons which kill insects

h. poisonous

i. material given in advance to a newspaper for publishing

j. pay

Reviewing the Case

Answer the following questions and share your answers with a partner.

1. What kind of people would use AgroWorld products?
2. Why did AgroWorld shut its Mexico City plant?
3. Why is AgroWorld opening a plant in Quito, Ecuador?
4. What is AgroWorld doing to prevent leakage from the plant?
5. How does the community feel about the AgroWorld plant?
6. Why is the PR person important to the success of AgroWorld?

Making Inferences

Answer the following questions and share your answers with a partner.

1. The following advertisement appeared in an international newspaper. Based on the case, explain why AgroWorld wants the person it hires to have each of the qualifications mentioned in the advertisement.

AGROWORLD

Come grow with us!

We are one of the world's largest producers of agricultural products. We are presently looking for a public relations person to serve as a national and international liaison to promote and represent our new plant outside of Quito, Ecuador. The successful candidate should have the following qualifications:

- five or more years' experience in an international organization
- excellent cross-cultural skills and cultural sensitivity
- excellent communication and interpersonal skills
- strong knowledge of technology related to the industry
- proven ability to write press releases and promotional pieces
- strong organizational skills: able to maintain an office and direct own staff

2. How important are cultural sensitivity and cross-cultural communication skills for this position? Why are they important?

3. Are there any other skills you think the candidate needs to have? What kind of personal and work-related background do you think the candidate should have? Explain your answers.

Problem Solving: Information Gap

AgroWorld has reviewed all the resumes and now has two final candidates. You and your classmates must decide which of these two candidates to hire.

Divide the class into groups: A and B. Group A reads Manju Jairam's profile in Appendix Activity 9. Group B reads Paul Fraser's profile in Appendix Activity 29. After reading the profiles, complete your part of the chart below. Next, find a partner from the other group and ask questions to complete the chart.

	Manju Jairam	Paul Fraser
Education		
Work Experience		
Skills and Accomplishments		
Personal		

Discussion

Go back to your groups, look at the completed chart, and answer the following.

1. For each candidate go through the job requirements listed in the advertisement. State if and how the person meets the requirements.
2. For each candidate go through the other skills and background you listed as important in Making Inferences. State if and how the person has the skills and background you listed.
3. Choose your candidate and explain the reasons for your choice. Share your answer with the class.

Written Reflection

A successful international businessperson must have many personal qualities that reflect his or her commitment to cultural awareness and understanding. How exactly can the qualities listed below help an international businessperson in relationships and experiences with people from other cultures?

- *Adaptability:* being at ease and comfortable in different environments
- *Flexibility:* being able and willing to change your ideas or plans even on very short notice
- *Tolerance for ambiguity:* being able to work in a situation where you feel information is not always complete or clear
- *Internationalism:* having a commitment to learning about and exploring other cultures

Write a short paper in which you discuss the importance of each quality and give an example of a business situation where it is useful. Before writing, think about your experiences and experiences you have heard of, as well as about some of the cases in this book. When you have finished, share your written reflection with the class.

AROUND THE WORLD

Company Training of the International Executive

Many companies are now helping their employees build their cross-cultural communication skills. These companies offer cultural training workshops and seminars. Each year more and more companies are offering this type of training. They realize the importance of preparing their employees for the very different and challenging international business world. The following activity will give you an idea of what these training seminars are.

You and your classmates are salespeople for a sports clothes manufacturer which has been very successful domestically, but has never had any success internationally. The president of your company would like to try the international market again. This time she would like to try exporting products to India. She would like to set up a training program for the sales team (you and your classmates). She has asked you to a meeting to discuss what type of overseas training you should receive. She has given you the following list of possible topics to be covered in a training program. The program is designed to help you prepare for both living and working in India. Unfortunately your company can offer only five workshops due to money problems.

POSSIBLE TRAINING PROGRAMS TO BE OFFERED

_____ History of India

_____ Indian Social Practices

_____ Hindi Language

_____ Indian Domestic Management Styles (management within Indian companies)

_____ Indian Economy

_____ Indian Distribution Practices (distribution of goods within India)

_____ Indian Negotiating Styles

_____ Indian Politics

_____ Indian Culture

_____ Legal Aspects of Indian Business

_____ Organization of Indian Business

_____ Culture Shock

Your Point of View

Which of the topics are most important for an overseas training program? On your own, decide which five topics are most important and rank those five topics in order of importance. 1 = most important. Then share your decisions in a small group. As a group, create one final list of five topics.

Discussion

The following bar graph shows how Japanese and non-Japanese (North American) businesspeople responded to a similar list of topics for a training program for businesspeople going to Japan to live and work. Study the graph carefully and answer the questions that follow.

Advice from the Field: Essential Training for Japanese Duty

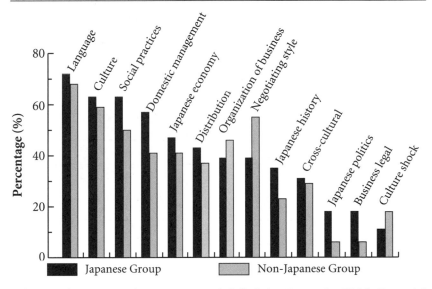

John Frankenstein and Hassan Hosseini, "Advice From the Field: Essential Training." Reprinted by permission of the publisher from *Management Review* (July 1988). © 1988 American Management Association, New York. All rights reserved.

1. a. What does the non-Japanese group feel is most important for an international businessperson to know when preparing for business in Japan? List the four most important topics.

   b. What does the Japanese group feel is most important for an international businessperson to learn when preparing for business in Japan? List the four most important topics.

   c. What are the main similarities and differences? What does this answer say about Western and Japanese styles of doing business?

2. In what ways are your choices of topics similar to the groups in the graphs? In what ways are they different? What does this say about your style of doing business?

3. What other topics can you think of that are not included in the lists that are also important?

Preparing Yourself   The previous exercise helped you to think about general topics you would like to learn more about when going overseas. The next exercise will help you to think about more specific issues.

Applying Your Knowledge

Before you go overseas on a business trip, you should prepare a list of questions you would like to have answered. For each topic listed below, think of at least two important questions. All the topics have been covered in this book. Feel free to refer to the previous chapters if needed. An example question is given for the first topic.

Initial Contacts

1. *Do we need a third-party introduction?*
2. _____

Gift Giving

1. _____
2. _____

Introductions/Names

1. _____
2. _____

Entertainment Practices

1. _____
2. _____

Use of Time

1. _____
2. _____

Negotiator Characteristics

1. _____
2. _____

Nonverbal Communication

1. _____
2. _____

Negotiating Process

   1. _____

   2. _____

Forms of Agreement

   1. _____

   2. _____

Use of Media

   1. _____

   2. _____

Management Styles

   1. _____

   2. _____

Class Presentations

Imagine that your classmates are going to your country to do business and that you must train them before they go. To do this, you will prepare an oral presentation focusing on business practices in your country and on the cultural values behind these practices. If you are in a monocultural classroom, you should choose a country that interests you, research the country, and prepare a presentation focusing on the business practices and cultural values of that country.

Presentation Guidelines

1. You must give your classmates all the important information they will need to be more comfortable and successful on their business trip.

2. Include information about the business culture as well as the country's basic data and information (e.g., size of country, economy, major exports and imports).

3. Be sure your presentation is well referenced by doing one or more of the following: (1) contacting one of the information sources listed on page 156; (2) talking to actual business people from your country; and (3) reading articles from magazines or books about your country. Provide your classmates and teacher with your references.

4. To help you organize the cultural part of your presentation, address the questions and topics from the previous Applying Your Knowledge activity. Present your country's basic information first, followed by the business information.

As you listen to each presentation, take notes and complete the following information sheet. Write three important pieces of basic information about the country, five important pieces of information about the business culture of the country, and three questions you have about the country that you would like the speaker to answer.

COUNTRY:

PRESENTER:

DATE:

Country Information:

1.

2.

3.

Business Culture Information:

1.

2.

3.

4.

5.

Three Questions I Would Like to Ask:

1.

2.

3.

LANGUAGE EXPANSION

Expressions and Idioms

We know that an international businessperson must be flexible, patient, and able to adapt to different environments. In the United States we have idioms that express these qualities.

Match the idioms to their definitions.

_____ 1. to play it (the situation) by ear

_____ 2. to ride out the storm

_____ 3. to go with the flow

_____ 4. to not rock the boat

_____ 5. to meet halfway

a. to accept a situation by not trying to change anything and letting the other person lead; to be patient and flexible

b. to not cause problems; to adapt

c. to wait and see how a situation progresses before making a decision; to make changes as you go along instead of going by a plan

d. to compromise; to be flexible

e. to not leave a situation that is unfavorable at present, but rather to wait for it to get better; to be patient

Substitute the words in italics with the idiom that would fit best in the context.

1. The import taxes were getting higher and higher each year. Even though the company suffered financially, its executive decided to *continue paying the high cost* because they knew eventually the cost would come down.

2. Before the meeting, Mr. Woodson was told to *keep his opinions to himself and not to disagree on any issue.*

3. The salesman wanted $7,500 for the car. The customer wanted to pay $6,500. They *bargained* and the customer paid $7,000.

4. In the beginning, we thought the meetings would only last two days. After two days, it was clear the meetings would go on for another week. Instead of trying to speed things up, we *accepted the extended schedule* and stayed for five more days.

5. The company could not decide between the Japanese and the Russian bid. Instead of going by their original plan, they decided *to wait until the last minute, then decide what to do.*

Word Forms

Often the same word base can be used in verb, noun, and adjective form. Complete the following chart with the missing verb or noun form.

Verb	Noun	Adjective
leak		leaky
	industry	industrialized
	acquisition	acquirable
incorporate		
	compensation	compensatory
prevent		preventable
	qualifier	qualified

Complete each sentence with the correct verb, noun, or adjective form. Use one form of each word base, and do not repeat any words.

1. The company _____ two smaller independent companies this year. This makes them the largest soft drink company in the market.

2. The _____ of computers in industry has been hard on factory workers. Many have lost their jobs to a computer.

3. The _____ warehouse roof caused extensive water damage. It will cost the company over $10,000 to replace the damaged goods.

4. The factory workers received some _____ for working longer hours during the Christmas holidays.

5. Unfortunately, Silvio did not _____ for the job. He could not type fast enough.

6. Raising the cost of the soft drink was not _____ . The raw goods used to make the drink doubled in price.

7. Most _____ countries have nuclear power facilities.

INFORMATION SOURCES FOR PROJECTS

Cultural Resource Centers:

Culturegrams

These are newsletters written for people traveling overseas. Topics are general and include customs and courtesies, the people, lifestyles, and the nation. There are culturegrams available for more than 100 areas of the world.

At the time of publication the cost was U.S. $1.00 for each culturegram.

To order a culturegram, you can call or write:

David M. Kennedy Center for International Studies
Publication Services
280 Herald R. Clark Building
Provo, Utah 84602
1-800-528-6279

United States Information Service (USIS) Libraries

These are libraries located around the world that provide English language business magazines, books, and other resources. Check with a U.S. embassy or consulate in your country for more information.

Business Resource Centers:

Consulates and Embassies

Many consulates and embassies are able to provide you with basic information about their countries. They may also suggest other agencies and information sources.

Chamber of Commerce of the United States

1615 H. St., N.W.
Washington D.C. 20062
(202) 463-5427

The chamber provides a list of publications covering many countries. In addition, it can connect you with American Chambers of Commerce overseas in many countries.

APPENDIX

1

Actual Case Ending the FII-Fyffes and Pernod-Ricard Disagreement

The Irish judge honored Pernod-Ricard's interpretation of the handshake. He said that Pernod-Ricard's actions during the negotiation were more consistent than those of FII-Fyffes. The Irish judge said, "I have no doubt that the negotiations had in this case, ripened [developed] into an agreement." In other words, the Irish judge believed Pernod-Ricard was correct and that FII-Fyffes did not act fairly.

2

Italian students said this about their own culture and U.S. Culture.

Our Country	The United States
family	hard work
romantic love	material success
enjoying life	independence
loyalty to others	privacy

Japanese students said this about their own culture and U.S. culture.

Our Country	The United States
honor in the community	material success
efficiency	enjoying life
formality	creativity
loyalty to others	informality

3

The Misunderstanding in the Singaporean–American Encounter

In the United States, the first name is a given name and the last name is the family name. So the businessman thought that Lo Win Hao's given name was Lo Win and that his family name was Hao. As a sign of respect he called the man by a title, Mr., with his last name, Hao.

In the Chinese tradition, the family name is first and the given name is second. So the American was calling his colleague by his personal given name, not his more formal family name. This is a very informal address and is not appropriate in first meetings for the Chinese in Singapore. In the Chinese tradition it is only appropriate to call a person by his given name when you know the person very well.

4

Group A: Seller's Information

Price per unit	$3.50 per widget
Conditions of assembly	Can ship in parts or ready assembled. Preferable to ship in parts and then send a supervisor to assist with assembly
Terms of payment	With prepayment get 10 percent discount. A letter of credit payment limited to sixty days
Delivery date	Can only provide 5,000 widgets by May. Other 5,000 widgets available in August
Future discounts	10% discount on repeat order
Other conditions	A minimum order of 2,500 widgets

5

Group B: U.S. Cultural Information

Telecommunications

In the United States phone communication is very common and accepted. Business meetings are frequently conducted on phones. Sometimes people work together for months or even years before ever meeting.

Introductions

In the United States one can use social connections to get introduced, but a social introduction is not as effective as it is in other countries. Doing a special favor for a friend is not a respected business practice. Introductions through trade associations are a fairly common practice. For salespeople it is even more common to directly introduce oneself without the help of a third party.

Representation

The character of a company is more important than the character of the person representing the company in the United States. The question one asks in the first contact is, "Can we do business with this company?" Businesspeople change jobs frequently. These frequent changes encourage U.S. business relationships to focus more on the companies than on the individuals representing the companies.

Personal Connections

Succeeding without the help of special personal connections shows independence and an ability to work hard. These qualities are highly respected. Working on your own does not hurt your reputation. As a matter of fact, the more powerful a person is, the more isolated the person can become.

Time

"Time is money" is a common saying in the United States. In making initial contacts, very little time is spent on building social relationships. Conversation is quickly focused on business. If there are any dinners or social events they are mainly used to discuss business, not other interests. The home office usually pressures the salesman to get the account as quickly as possible.

6

Arrival Times: One American's Response

Event	Arrival Time
a. A doctor's appointment for 8:30 A.M.	8:20–8:25 A.M.
b. A class that begins at 2:00 P.M.	1:50–1:55 P.M.
c. A business meeting set for 3:30 P.M.	3:25 P.M.
d. Your job that starts at 9:00 A.M.	9:00 A.M.
e. A train that is scheduled to leave at 7:17 P.M.	7:00 P.M.
f. A dinner party at a friend's house set for. 6:30 P.M.	6:30–6:40 P.M.

7

Group B: Letter from Mr. Pablo Arango to His Boss, Mr. José González

Dear Mr. González,

I hope that this letter finds you and your lovely family in good health. As you have asked, I am writing you to tell you about the recent happenings at the Tijuana factory and my feelings about them. As I said, it has been quite a struggle adjusting to our new manager, and I hope you can give me some advice as to how to handle the situation.

One of my biggest problems with Ms. Graus is that she is very unfriendly with the workers. She does not approve of me socializing at work with the workers. She says that it is not professional to talk with them about personal matters or do them personal favors. I don't agree. If an employee has a problem, it directly affects their work. Also, I believe that workers will only trust and respect a boss who helps them with their problems and shows interest in them as people, not just as workers.

Another problem is that the floor supervisors find Ms. Graus too controlling. She has them working on projects with which she gives them little information. They are not involved at all in the decision-making process; she simply gives them orders. Ten years ago this type of management would have been acceptable. These days my supervisors want to have more responsibility for their projects. I believe that the more they are asked for their opinions and ideas, the better job they will do. They will have a personal interest in the work which they have helped to develop. I have to say that not all that Ms. Graus does is horrible. She tried to raise the employees' morale by organizing a competition. Bonuses were to be given to the workers whose output for the week was greatest. I tried to explain to her that *all* the employees needed more money and that a competition was not the way to raise company morale. Our employees do not want to work in an environment where they are asked to compete against one another. This creates distrust and disharmony among the workers. Needless to say, there was no great increase in anyone's output.

These are most of the major issues. I hope that you can help me with some of them. I will continue to do my best, although at times it can be very difficult. Please send my fondest regards to your family.

8

Group A: Colombian Cultural Information

Telecommunications

In Colombia, the phone is not used as much as it is in information-centered cultures like the United States. Important business is taken care of in person or on paper. A phone call is an inappropriate way to introduce oneself or sell something.

Introductions

One can introduce oneself or go through an agency in Colombia, but the most effective way to be introduced is through a common friend or contact. It is very important to be well connected to decision makers.

Representation

The character of the person who represents a business is more important than the character of the business he represents. This means that in the initial contact the most commonly asked question is: "Can I do business with this person?", not "Can we do business with this company?" Business relationships operate on a personal level and last a longer time than in the United States.

Personal Connections

In Colombia, the better connected a person is to important decision makers, the more attractive he or she is as a business partner. The more associations a person has, the more power that person has.

Time

Because personal relationships are important in business in Colombia, one expects to spend some time in the beginning to get to know each other. Trust and loyalty are the foundation of a good business relationship. They don't develop in a day. In the first contact, time is spent getting to know each other. A dinner talking about general interests, not about business, is a common way to begin a business relationship. The relationship may develop with small favors, frequent visits, and time.

9

Group A: Manju Jairam's Profile

She graduated from Oxford University in London with an advanced degree in international business (1980). Since graduation she has been working for an international pesticide company in London. She started her career in marketing and is now the manager of the entire marketing division. Her division handles all marketing and promotion within the European Economic Community.

As marketing manager, she was able to resolve a long-term dispute between the company's French and German subsidiaries. She also reorganized the marketing department during a financial crisis, which saved the company a great deal of money. Her marketing and promotional campaigns have won many international awards.

Manju was born in England to Indian parents. She is not married. She speaks English and Hindi fluently and has studied French and German in the university.

10

The Misunderstanding in the Saudi-German Encounter

Three of Johann's actions offended Bouchaib. First of all, Johann had brought a bottle of Scotch and cookies. Bouchaib is a devout Muslim. According to his religion he must not drink alcohol. Also, in Persian Gulf states, bringing a gift of food and drink implies the host isn't generous enough to offer his own food and drink.

Second, in Saudi Arabia it is customary to refuse an offer a few times before accepting. Johann seemed greedy to accept Bouchaib's offer of coffee so quickly.

Finally, Johann refused Bouchaib's gift of the book. In Bouchaib's eyes, by refusing his gift, Johann was refusing his offer of friendship.

11

Group B: Japanese Cultural Information

Phases of Negotiation

The negotiation process can be divided into four phases: 1) building a good relationship; 2) talking about the business deal; 3) persuading, bargaining, and making concessions; and 4) making a final agreement. In Japan the first two phases take the longest, especially since personal trust and mutual understanding are important to good business relationships. Thus the last two phases, bargaining and final agreements, come at the end of a long process of building a relationship and talking about the proposed deal.

Concessions

In Japan concessions are made only at the end of the negotiation process. After all the possible details of the business deal have been carefully discussed, the two parties begin to bargain and make concessions. They quickly come to a final agreement.

Contracts

Contracts do not play a central role in negotiations in Japan. In fact, a contract is usually a small detail at the end of a long process of negotiation. After all aspects of the deal have been discussed and all decisions have been made verbally, a contract is written up reflecting the decisions. A contract is presented at a meeting only after both parties have carefully discussed the final agreement.

Long-Term vs. Short-Term Planning

Businesses have traditionally focused on long-term business projects. Many projects are begun with the knowledge that they will not produce profits for years. Much time is spent developing a strong and stable business relationship and planning a good partnership. This planning will benefit both parties in the long term.

12

The Solution

c. The Italian and Swiss teams decided to live for a short period of time in each other's countries. In this way they could learn to appreciate the time value differences in each country and learn more about each other's cultures.

13

Project 2 — Paper Boxes

You will be a *laissez faire* manager. In other words, aside from giving your workers their basic task, you will not tell them what to do. The workers will decide everything for themselves.

Tell your workers: Use your paper and tape to make paper boxes. You will decide as a group how to make the boxes. Work together and listen to one another's ideas and opinions. I'll check your boxes in ten minutes. I know you'll do a good job.

After you give the instructions, sit to the side and do not involve yourself in the project. If the workers are having problems, have them solve their problems without you.

14

Group A: Letter from Ms. Mara Graus to Her Boss in Germany, Dr. Sigmund Heinz

Dear Dr. Heinz,

Please excuse the lateness of this letter as I know I should have written sooner. Everything here in Mexico is going along a little slower than I had hoped. Mr. Arango and I are having some disagreements over management issues. I hope you will send me some advice for resolving some of these problems.

One of the biggest problems is that Mr. Arango spends a lot of time on the floor socializing with the workers, joking around with them, and asking about their families and their personal problems. He also insists on helping them with personal favors. I feel that the workers are not taking their jobs seriously because of the relaxed and social atmosphere he creates. I have spoken with him about this issue, but he insists on keeping close relationships with the workers. I tried to tell him that workers respect a manager who works hard and has great technical ability.

On the issue of control and management, Mr. Arango has asked that I give the floor supervisors more responsibility and control. He feels that they are not involved enough in the decision-making process and that they should receive more information about their projects. I believe I have given them the information they need to do their work. In addition, I am their boss and they should not have to worry about all the details. That is my job, and what I get paid for. They should trust me and my decisions.

In the middle of all these problems, I thought the workers needed to have something to raise their morale. I came up with the idea of having a competition for the factory. It was very simple: each week the employee who produced the greatest output would get a bonus. I was sure that this would be very popular, although Mr. Arango disagreed with me. I believe that competition is a great motivational tool and leads to new ideas in efficiency and production. Unfortunately, here at the factory there was no change in output.

Well, as you can see, I am very disappointed by the way things are going. I realize that this is my first overseas assignment and that I should be happy to have such an important position. In truth, this is the most difficult position I have had. I would appreciate any help or advice you can give me.

15

Group B: Buyer's Information

Price per unit	$3.00 per widget
Conditions of assembly	Prefer ready assembled, not in parts
Terms of payment	Want to pay over six months with a letter of credit
Delivery date	Need 1,500 widgets by May. If satisfied with the product, will repeat order of 5,000 for July
Future discounts	Want a 15 percent discount on the repeat order
Other conditions	Want only 1,500 widgets in first order

16

Manager A: Project 1 — Paper Sailing Ships

You will be an *autocratic* manager. In other words, you will make all decisions and tell your workers exactly what to do.

First read the instructions for making the paper ships to yourself and make sure you understand them. Ask your teacher for help if there is anything you do not understand. Then read each step to the workers. Do not go on to the next step until all workers have completed the step. Always stay in control of the workers. Never ask for suggestions, and ignore any suggestions the workers give you. After each step, look at all the workers' projects and correct any mistakes.

Materials: a sheet of paper

Instructions:

1. Fold a piece of paper in half the long way.
2. Open the paper and fold it in half the short way.
3. Take one of the two corners along the fold and fold it down at an angle toward the center crease. Do the same with the other folded corner.
4. Turn up the bottom piece toward the top. Turn over and repeat on the other side. You should now have a triangle shape.
5. Press the two end points of the triangle together at the bottom so that the middle creases become the outside folds. You should now have a diamond shape.
6. Fold the bottom point of the diamond up to the top point of the diamond. Turn over and repeat on the other side. You should now have a triangle shape.
7. Again press the two end points of the triangle together at the bottom so that the middle creases become the outside folds. You should now have a diamond shape.
8. At the top of your folded diamond, three corner points come together to form one corner. Hold the two outside points and pull them away from the middle point. Press down on the sides to complete your boat.

17

Group A: Pernod-Ricard's Position

Make a speech to defend your position. Consider the following points.

1. You made an offer of $4.50. The FII-Fyffes representative considered the price acceptable.
2. At the end of the meeting you shook hands on the $4.50 per share with the FII-Fyffes representative. This handshake meant that you had both agreed on the offer.
3. In your country a handshake is a binding form of agreement.
4. FII-Fyffes finalized the agreement and must therefore honor it.

18

Group A: Italian Cultural Information

Tasks in a Polychronic Culture

Italian people are said to belong to a generally polychronic culture (although not all people are exclusively polychronic). *Polychronic* means many or multiple times. Polychronic people are used to doing several tasks at the same time. They do not have to complete one task before beginning the next. Instead, they can flow back and forth between tasks easily. As they work on one task, they may decide to go back and change parts of a previous task.

Schedules and Deadlines

In a polychronic culture, the future tends to be seen as unpredictable so that tight schedules are considered difficult and impractical. Therefore, schedules are often flexible to allow for unforseeable interruptions and changes in plans. People understand that delays are a part of life and are necessary for developing the best possible product or service. They would rather spend more time perfecting a product or service than meeting a deadline.

19

The Misunderstanding in the American–Japanese Encounter

In Japan, silence can be part of a conversation. If someone wants to think about an offer, silence gives that person time to consider it carefully. In the United States people are rarely silent in conversation. Silence is considered to be a negative response to an offer. The Americans in this case thought the Japanese were unhappy with the offer, so they lowered the price. The Japanese team did not know that the American team was expecting an immediate response to the offer.

20

Manager C: Project 3 — Paper Hats

You will be a *democratic* manager. In other words, you will be in control of the project and make suggestions, but you will ask the workers for their suggestions and opinions. You will use the suggestions that you feel are the best for the project.

First read the instructions for making paper hats to yourself and make sure you understand them. Ask your teacher for help if there is anything you do not understand.

Then tell your workers that they are going to make hats and ask, "Does anyone know how to make paper hats?" Encourage all workers to participate and share ideas on how to make hats. Decide if these ideas are better than the instructions below. If they are not, thank the group but use the instructions below. If the suggestions are better, use the workers' ideas. In either case, remember to stay in control and make all final decisions, but also encourage the group to continue making suggestions.

Materials: a sheet of paper and a pair of scissors

Instructions:

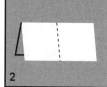
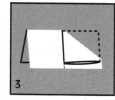
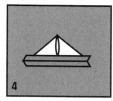
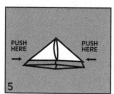

1. Fold a piece of paper in half the long way.
2. Open the paper and fold it in half the short way.
3. Take one of the two corners along the fold and fold it into the center crease. Do the same with the other corner.
4. Turn up the end flaps.
5. Cut the corners off the flaps.

21

Group A: Nigerian Cultural Information

Nigeria and Negotiators

In Nigeria, the age of the negotiator is extremely important because age means wisdom and reflects status and importance. To send a young negotiator means you are not seriously interested in the negotiation. If you are interested, you will send a person with authority and seniority. A good educational background is also highly respected and important. Nigerians also put great importance on formality and social skills. The sex of the negotiator is not very important, since many Nigerian women run their own businesses. In addition, Nigerian businessmen are generally aware of the role of American women in management. In Nigeria, negotiating in groups is common.

22

Group A : French Cultural Information

Social Classes

In France there is some emphasis on class differences. People usually do not socialize across social and economic classes. Different levels of the company, such as secretarial and executive levels, are associated with different classes. So, in office life, secretaries and executives are not expected to socialize together.

The Role of the Boss in Office Life

The boss represents authority. The boss should not be too casual or social with his employees. If the boss is too relaxed, the employees lose their respect for his or her authority.

Entertaining

In France, the home is a private place where only close friends or family are invited. Business colleagues usually socialize in restaurants or other public places.

Business entertainment is very different from social entertainment. It is much more formal. It is usually limited to a business lunch or dinner in a restaurant. For social entertainment, the French rarely throw parties. It is much more common to have a small dinner party where everyone sits down together to eat. The informal come-and-go style of a party is not popular.

23

Group B: U.S. Cultural Information

United States and Negotiators

In the United States, sending a person with great technical competence and knowledge to negotiate is most important. It shows you are serious about negotiations because you are sending an employee who is ready to answer any product questions. Power and authority are important but are more the result of your talent and work record than of your age or seniority in the company. The sex of the negotiator is not important since many women occupy professional and managerial positions. North Americans are accustomed to sending only one person. Sometimes this is called the "John Wayne approach." This means that the individual thinks he or she can handle the negotiation on his or her own; it reflects the strong individualism found among North Americans.

24

Group B: U.S. Cultural Information

Social Classes

In the United States, differences in social and economic classes exist, but are not emphasized. Although colleagues from different classes may not socialize together frequently, there usually is at least one annual event where all employees come together. The most common events are Christmas parties and company picnics. Because equality is so highly valued in the United States, formal situations that emphasize class differences are avoided. Social events are usually casual and relaxed.

The Role of the Boss in Office Life

The boss has authority but should not abuse it. As much as possible, the boss should just be one of the workers. For this reason American bosses are usually casual and informal with their employees. Because it is believed that good social relationships build a good work environment, bosses often throw parties to build a sense of unity among the employees and to strengthen employee identity with the company.

Entertaining

It is common in the U.S. to invite business colleagues or other acquaintances home for a dinner party or cocktail party. The home is a place of hospitality and entertainment.

In the U.S., there is not a big difference between how people socialize with colleagues and with friends. Both kinds of socializing are informal and relaxed. The party is a popular way of entertaining. Instead of a formal dinner at a table, often Americans entertain with an informal buffet or just cocktails and a snack. In addition to parties, common social activities include playing sports, going out for drinks after work, and going to sports or cultural events.

25

Group A: U.S. Cultural Information

Phases of Negotiation

The negotiation process can be divided into four phases: 1) building a good relationship; 2) talking about the business deal; 3) persuasion, bargaining, and making concessions; and 4) making a final agreement. In the United States, the first two phases are not emphasized, because personal relationships do not play a large role in business life and because making a quick deal is important. The negotiation process soon moves to the last two phases as bargaining and making a final agreement are the focus of negotiations.

Concessions

Concessions are made during most of the negotiation process. At the beginning, while the two parties are talking about the proposed deal, small concessions are given to show cooperation. As the two parties continue to talk about each issue of business, they bargain and make concessions. The bargaining continues issue by issue until the final agreement is signed. Each concession is met with a concession from the other party. In this way, the two parties treat each other as equals and demonstrate a cooperative attitude and a commitment to the negotiations.

(continued on next page)

Contracts

The contract is a tool in the negotiation process. It is a working document that will be changed during negotiations. It is usually introduced in the second phase of negotiations and is discussed throughout the rest of the process. Presenting a contract at a meeting shows that a party is committed to the deal and is ready to think about the details of the agreement.

Long-Term vs. Short-Term Planning

Companies in the United States traditionally have focused on short-term business deals. For example, if a business relationship does not bring immediate profits, the companies involved might end the relationship rather than waiting to see if the situation changes for the better. In view of this short-term business focus, it does not make sense for companies to spend a long time in negotiations.

26

Product Market

Who eats peanuts in your country? If no one, who eats products similar to peanuts?

When and where are they eaten?

Product Image

What image do peanuts have in your country?

Is the image good for sales or not?

If not, how can you change the image to improve sales?

Flavor of Product

Do you like the flavor of plain peanuts?

How would you change the flavor to adapt to tastes in your country?

How many and what flavors should be offered?

Package

Is the Good Earth package attractive to you?

Is the 100 gram package a good size for retail sales?

How would you adapt the package to make it more attractive?

Medium of Promotion

Do you think you can reach peanut consumers best on radio, TV, or in a print medium such as magazines or newspapers?

Message in Promotion

What message do you think will persuade your target audience to buy your product?

27

Group B: FII-Fyffes's Position

Make a speech to defend your position. Consider the following points.

1. You agreed that $4.50 per share was a good offer.
2. At the end of the meeting you shook hands with the Pernod-Ricard representative, but for you the handshake just meant the meeting was over.
3. In your country written agreements, not handshakes, are considered binding. You never signed anything.
4. You did not finalize the agreement with Pernod-Ricard, and therefore are free to consider offers from other companies.

28

Group B: Swiss Cultural Information

Tasks in a Monochronic Culture

Swiss people are said to belong to a monochronic culture (although not all people are exclusively monochronic). *Monochronic* means "single time." Time is divided into segments that are measured by the clock. Tasks are assigned to each of these segments and so are given a limited amount of time. Usually, each task is finished before the next task is begun. It is not easy for a monochronic person to return to a task once it has been completed.

Schedules and Deadlines

In a monochronic culture, future time is predictable and carefully planned. Scheduling events means that each segment of time is carefully arranged. If extra time is needed, this will interfere with plans for the next time segment. Breaking schedules and deadlines affects future schedules and deadlines. This can have negative effects on relations with those people or companies who are asked to delay their plans and change their schedules.

29

Group B: Paul Fraser's Profile

Paul graduated from the University of Massachusetts in the United States with an undergraduate degree in Spanish (1981). After graduation he taught high school Spanish and at the same time completed a degree in engineering. He then worked for the Peace Corps in Guatemala for two years. For the past four years he has been working for the World Health Organization.

His accomplishments include assisting in the design and implementation of a modern sewage (waste) treatment plant in a remote area of Peru. His responsibilities during this project included working with local politicians, businesspeople, and public health people to keep the cost of the sewage treatment system low. He also gave fund raising speeches raising over $200,000 to help with the cost of the plant. After the project was completed, he stayed to help run the plant.

Paul was born in the United States. His mother is Colombian, and he lived in Colombia for ten years during his childhood. He is married to a Peruvian woman, has two children, and speaks Spanish fluently.

30

The Top Ten World Brands

Listed in order of success. (From *The Marketing Challenge* by Laura Mazur and Annik Hogg. England: Addison Wesley, 1993.)

1. Coca Cola
2. Kellogg's
3. McDonald's
4. Kodak
5. Marlboro
6. IBM
7. American Express
8. Sony
9. Mercedes-Benz
10. Nescafé

ANSWER KEY

Unit 1

Vocabulary

1. h **2.** i **3.** j **4.** e **5.** f **6.** c **7.** b **8.** a
9. d **10.** g

Applying Your Knowledge

1. S **2.** G **3.** G **4.** S **5.** G **6.** G **7.** S
8. G **9.** S **10.** S

Expressions and Idioms

1. c **2.** a **3.** b **4.** e **5.** d

1. catch on
2. is beyond
3. hear someone out
4. see
5. read between the lines

Word Forms

Verb	Noun	Adjective
behave	*behavior*	
collaborate	collaboration	collaborative
consider	*consideration*	considered
frustrate	frustration	frustrated
generalize	*generalization*	generalized
prejudge	*prejudice*	prejudiced
respond	*response*	responsive
tense	*tension*	tense

1. behavior **2.** tense **3.** consider **4.** frustrate **5.** collaborate
6. respond **7.** generalize **8.** Prejudice

Unit 2

Vocabulary

1. c **2.** a **3.** b **4.** c **5.** a **6.** c **7.** a **8.** b
9. b **10.** a **11.** c **12.** c

Expressions and Idioms

1. a **2.** c **3.** b **4.** e **5.** d

1. warmed up to
2. get to know
3. hit it off
4. get along with
5. to break the ice

Word Forms

Verb	Noun	Adjective
adapt	*adaptation*	adaptable
contact	*contact*	contacted
accustom (oneself)	*custom*	customary
impress	impression	impressive
inform	information	informative
introduce	*introduction*	introductory
refer	reference	referred
	reputation	reputable

1. contact **2.** customs **3.** impress **4.** introductory **5.** references
6. adaptable **7.** information **8.** reputation

Unit 3

Vocabulary

1. b   2. a   3. b   4. c   5. c   6. b   7. a   8. a
9. c   10. b

Expressions and Idioms

1. b   2. d   3. a   4. e   5. c

1. It's on us/me.
2. went out on the town
3. wined and dined
4. took (them) out to
5. token of their appreciation

Word Forms

Verb	Noun	Adjective
accept	acceptance	acceptable
get acquainted with	*acquaintance*	acquainted
appreciate	*appreciation*	appreciative
compliment	*compliment*	complimentary
entertain	*entertainment*	entertaining
	hospitality	hospitable
invite	*invitation*	invited
socialize	socializing	social

1. appreciation   2. get acquainted with   3. compliment
4. invitation   5. Socializing   6. acceptable   7. entertain
8. hospitality

Unit 4

Vocabulary

1. h   2. k   3. i   4. f   5. e   6. j   7. c   8. a
9. d   10. g   11. b

Expressions and Idioms

1. budget   2. losing   3. have invested   4. give
5. have spent   6. save

Word Forms

Verb	Noun	Adjective
schedule	*schedule*	scheduled
modify	modification	modified
	punctuality	punctual
predict	prediction	predictable
measure	measurement	*measurable*
warehouse	warehouse	
specify	specification	specific
communicate	*communication*	communicative

1. measurements   2. Punctuality   3. warehouses   4. scheduling
5. communication   6. to predict   7. specified   8. modified

Unit 5

Vocabulary

1. e 2. f 3. b 4. c 5. a 6. d 7. g 8. h

Expressions and Idioms

1. f 2. e 3. d 4. c 5. b 6. a

1. home court advantage
2. opponent
3. warm up the opponent
4. set the ground rules
5. game plan
6. struck out

Word Forms

Verb	Noun	Adjective
	competence	competent
know	*knowledge*	knowledgeable
authorize	authority	authorized
	ambition	ambitious
compete	*competition*	competitive
create	*creation*	creative
train	training	trainable
persuade	*persuasion*	persuasive

1. authorize 2. training 3. To compete 4. persuasive
5. create 6. ambitious 7. knowledge 8. competent

Unit 6

Vocabulary

1. b 2. a 3. a 4. b 5. c 6. a 7. a 8. b
9. b 10. b

Expressions and Idioms

1. d 2. b 3. e 4. c 5. a

1. lay all the cards on the table
2. has a card up his sleeve
3. has a poker face
4. closed the deal
5. stacked the deck

Word Forms

Verb	Noun	Adjective
arrange	*arrangement*	arranged
bargain	*bargain*	
commit	commitment	committed
concede	concession	concessionary
process	*process*	processed
profit	*profit*	profitable
propose	*proposal*	proposed

1. committed 2. process 3. profits 4. proposed 5. bargains
6. conceded 7. arranged

Unit 7

Vocabulary

1. c 2. b 3. a 4. b 5. b 6. b 7. c 8. c

Expressions and Idioms

1. d 2. c 3. b 4. a 5. f 6. e

1. give you my word of honor
2. lived up to his word
3. go back on my word
4. take him at his word
5. have the last word

Word Forms

Verb	Noun	Adjective
assess	assessment	assessable
detail	detail	detailed
emphasize	*emphasis*	emphatic
oblige	*obligation*	obligatory
predict	prediction	predictable
transact	*transaction*	transactional
finalize	final	final
bind	bind	binding

1. predictable 2. emphasis 3. final 4. detailed 5. assesses
6. obligation 7. bind 8. transactions

Unit 8

Vocabulary

1. j 2. i 3. d 4. h 5. e 6. c 7. g 8. f
9. a 10. b

Expressions and Idioms

1. b 2. c 3. e 4. a 5. d

1. buyer's market
2. on the market
3. flea markets
4. play the market
5. in the market for

Word Forms

Verb	Noun	Adjective
prohibit	*prohibition*	prohibited
promote	promotion	promotional
consume	consumer	consumable
restrict	*restriction*	restrictive
standardize	standard	standard
target	*target*	targeted

1. standardize 2. prohibited 3. consumers 4. target
5. promoted 6. restrictions

Unit 9

Vocabulary

1. f **2.** a **3.** e **4.** i **5.** d **6.** c **7.** g **8.** b
9. h

Expressions and Idioms

1. c **2.** e **3.** f **4.** b **5.** d **6.** a

1. Chris was a gatekeeper.
2. Paula was a tap dancer.
3. Harold was a blocker.
4. Andrew was a driver.
5. Shari was a harmonizer.
6. Steven was a fence sitter.

Word Forms

Verb	Noun	Adjective
adjust	*adjustment*	adjustable
supervise	supervisor	*supervisory*
satisfy	satisfaction	satisfactory
subordinate	*subordinate*	
dominate	domination	dominating/ dominant
motivate	*motivation*	motivational
consult	consultant	consulting

1. dominant **2.** supervisors **3.** to motivate/motivating
4. adjusting **5.** subordinates **6.** consulted **7.** satisfactory

Unit 10

Vocabulary

1. f **2.** g **3.** h **4.** d **5.** j **6.** c **7.** b **8.** e
9. a **10.** i

Expressions and Idioms

1. c **2.** e **3.** a **4.** b **5.** d

1. ride out the storm
2. not rock the boat
3. met halfway
4. went with the flow
5. play it by ear

Word Forms

Verb	Noun	Adjective
leak	*leakage*	leaky
industrialize	industry	industrialized
acquire	acquisition	acquirable
incorporate	*incorporation*	
compensate	compensation	compensatory
prevent	*prevention*	preventable
qualify	qualifier	qualified

1. acquired **2.** incorporation **3.** leaky **4.** compensation
5. qualify **6.** preventable **7.** industrialized